From Vision to Folly in the American Soul

I0123528

In *From Vision to Folly in the American Soul*, Thomas Singer collates his investigations into soul, both in its personal and collective manifestations.

With selected essays from twenty years of writing about American politics in the context of contemporary cultural trends, the book as a whole depicts an ongoing exploration of the complex relationships between individual and collective psyche in which reality, illusion, vision, and folly get all mixed up in overlapping political, cultural, and psychological conflicts.

This text is a valuable resource for academics and students of Jungian and post-Jungian ideas, politics, sociology, and American studies as well as for anyone interested in the current state of the United States.

Thomas Singer, MD, is a psychiatrist and Jungian psychoanalyst who trained at Yale Medical School, Dartmouth Medical School, and the C. G. Jung Institute of San Francisco. He is the author of many books and articles that include a series of books on cultural complexes that have focused on Australia, Latin America, Europe, the United States, and Far East Asian countries, in addition to another series of books featuring *Ancient Greece, Modern Psyche*. He serves on the board of ARAS (Archive for Research into Archetypal Symbolism) and has served as co-editor of *ARAS Connections* for many years.

Routledge Focus on Jung, Politics and Culture

The Jung, Politics and Culture series showcases the 'political turn' in Jungian and Post-Jungian psychology. Established and emerging authors offer unique perspectives and new insights as they explore the connections between Jungian psychology and key topics – including national and international politics, gender, race and human rights.

Titles in the series:

From Vision to Folly in the American Soul: Jung, Politics and Culture
Thomas Singer

Vision, Reality and Complex: Jung, Politics and Culture
Thomas Singer

For a full list of titles in this series, please visit www.routledge.com/
Focus-on-Jung-Politics-and-Culture/book-series/FJPC

From Vision to Folly
in the American Soul

Jung, Politics and Culture

Thomas Singer

Routledge
Taylor & Francis Group

LONDON AND NEW YORK

First published 2021
by Routledge
2 Park Square, Milton Park, Abingdon, Oxon OX14 4RN

and by Routledge
52 Vanderbilt Avenue, New York, NY 10017

Routledge is an imprint of the Taylor & Francis Group, an informa business

© 2021 Thomas Singer

The right of Thomas Singer to be identified as author of this work has been asserted by him in accordance with sections 77 and 78 of the Copyright, Designs and Patents Act 1988.

All rights reserved. No part of this book may be reprinted or reproduced or utilised in any form or by any electronic, mechanical, or other means, now known or hereafter invented, including photocopying and recording, or in any information storage or retrieval system, without permission in writing from the publishers.

Trademark notice: Product or corporate names may be trademarks or registered trademarks, and are used only for identification and explanation without intent to infringe.

British Library Cataloguing-in-Publication Data
A catalogue record for this book is available from the British Library

Library of Congress Cataloging-in-Publication Data
Names: Singer, Thomas, 1942– author.
Title: From vision to folly in the American soul : Jung, politics and culture / Thomas Singer.
Description: 1 Edition. | New York : Routledge, 2020. | Series: Focus on Jung, politics and culture | Includes bibliographical references and index.
Identifiers: LCCN 2020033649 (print) | LCCN 2020033650 (ebook) | ISBN 9780367432652 (hardback) | ISBN 9781003002208 (ebook)
Subjects: LCSH: Social psychology. | Jungian psychology. | Intergroup relations—United States. | Personality and culture—United States. | Psychoanalysis and culture.
Classification: LCC HM1033 .S546 2020 (print) | LCC HM1033 (ebook) | DDC 302—dc23
LC record available at https://lccn.loc.gov/2020033649
LC ebook record available at https://lccn.loc.gov/2020033650

ISBN: 978-0-367-43265-2 (hbk)
ISBN: 978-1-003-00220-8 (ebk)

Typeset in Times New Roman
by Apex CoVantage, LLC

I dedicate this book to Andrew Samuels with respect, admiration, and love. He has been an inspiration in exploring the boundaries between a psychological attitude and political activism. This book would simply not exist without Andrew's initiative in so many areas, not the least of which is the creation of the Routledge series on Jung, Politics and Culture.

Contents

Figures

Acknowledgments

LeeAnn Pickrell's care in fitting all the pieces of this book together goes way beyond professionalism. She is an artist in her way of knowing how to bring a complicated project to fruition – from the smallest detail to the broadest concept. And she is a joy to work with.

Introduction

When I was invited to gather a collection of papers for the Routledge Focus series, I was both honored and uncertain. I was not at all sure whether any coherence or overall meaning in the selection of papers would emerge. What actually happened in the process of puzzling together the different pieces of this collection was quite unexpected. I found that two separate but interrelated threads of inquiry came into perspective for me. As a result, I have ended up with two books, not one. The first book focuses on *Vision, Reality, and Complex*; it centers around the development of the cultural complex theory and explores the relationship between vision and reality in politics and psyche. The second book takes as its central theme *From Vision to Folly in the American Soul*. The essays in this book are more personal and inquire about soul both in its personal and collective manifestations.

In my writings, I have found an arc or trajectory as my attitude has changed over time. When I began to write about the relationships between psyche, politics, and culture, I felt it important to maintain a psychological objectivity, or "psychological attitude," as Joe Henderson called it. This seemed particularly important in trying not to identify too strongly with one side or another in conflicting political positions, which are often where cultural complexes express themselves. But, as time went on, my voice has become more personal, and I have become less reluctant to state my own point of view while hoping to maintain some psychological objectivity.

This book begins with "A Personal Meditation on Politics and the American Soul," which was published in 2007. At the time, I felt a bit like a fool in daring to speak about soul and politics, particularly when American automobile companies were staking claim to the soul as their own possession in advertisements for their cars, and US politics was on the way to selling its soul to *Citizens United* (2010), the Supreme Court decision that decided a corporation had the same free-speech rights as a person. The essay probes the relationship between one's personal soul journey and the soul journey of a nation, with the assumption that soul can be both individual and collective. I suggest in the second part of the essay that the soul of a nation is forged in the ways in which a country deals (or doesn't deal) with its cultural complexes. By the time I wrote the final contribution to this volume, which first appeared in 2019 in the third volume of the *Ancient Greece, Modern Psyche* series that I co-edited, I found myself embracing quite a different attitude from one of "psychological objectivity." Rather, "folly" presented itself to me as perhaps one of the few attitudes that makes sense in a world that has been making less and less sense to me.

Over time, the arc of my focus had shifted from vision and reality to folly, although vision and folly can often get quite entangled with one another and it can be hard to know which is which. Folly certainly has had her fans through the ages, and perhaps part of her attraction to me at this stage of my life, as I near my 80th year, is simply a function of my growing older. But certainly, the embrace of folly as a psychological attitude is also a function of the particularly disturbing times we are living in. Whatever the cause of this evolution in my own perspective, the trajectory from the first essay, on "A Personal Meditation on Politics and the American Soul," to the last essay, on "A Fool's Guide to Folly," has been as much an ongoing exploration of the relationships between reality, illusion, vision, and folly as the exploration of the relationships between psyche, politics, and culture. What I can say with some certainty at this point is that folly loves the splits between illusion, vision, and reality. A sense of folly permits us to tolerate and even laugh at what is otherwise unbearable and ridiculous – a challenge that faces many of us daily, both in the United States and in the rest of the world. And the positive side of folly allows us to plunge into life even as reason might warn us of its dangers. As Jung said, "Do you believe, man of this time, that laughter is lower than worship? Where is your measure, false measurer? The sum of life decides in laughter and in worship, not in your judgement."[1]

Dear readers

Because there is a limitation on the number of images that can be included in a print text, I have created a special arrangement with ARAS (the Archive for Research in Archetypal Symbolism) that permits me to link the reader to more images that add greatly to the written text. ARAS has graciously set up a special place on their website for readers to access these images and film clips, which can be reached simply by typing on a computer the URL link indicated at the appropriate places in the text: **https://aras.org/vision-folly-american-soul**. Once readers arrive at the ARAS file hosting this feature, they will be able to view the specific image according to chapter location.

Note

1 C. G. Jung, *The Red Book: A Reader's Edition*, ed. Sonu Shamdasani, trans. Sonu Shamdasani, Mark Kyburz, and John Peck (New York: W. W. Norton & Co., 2012), 122.

1   A personal meditation on politics and the American soul

From *Spring Journal* 78, 2007.[1]

In 2007, I was invited by Nancy Cater of Spring *Journal to contribute an article on politics and the soul of America to a special edition she was publishing. With the 2008 US presidential elections on the horizon, I approached the subject by suggesting that the emerging theory of cultural complexes on which I was elaborating might be one way to think about how the soul of America gets forged in the crucible of the interactions between psyche and politics. I outlined seven potent cultural complexes that stream through the American collective psyche from generation to generation. These same currents are at the core of the new 2020 Routledge book,* Cultural Complexes and the Soul of America.

An invitation to write about politics and the American soul should cause anyone with common sense to turn and run in the opposite direction, in the same way that seeing an advertisement for the "soul of a BMW" or hearing Cadillac's newly trademarked slogan – Life. Liberty. And The Pursuit. – induces nausea. The language of soul and politics has been so co-opted by a vast public-relations machine, which instantaneously turns everything, including soul, into a marketable commodity, that there are probably only a handful of us foolish enough to tackle the subject.

The purpose of this essay is to be more impressionistic and evocative than precisely descriptive of the relationship between the American soul and politics – partly because it is so hard to give specific definitions to such essentially indefinable realities. It may be helpful to think of soul as having both a function and a content. As a function and not a specific content, we experience soul as emotional, embodied psychic movement.

Soul, as a function of psychic movement, can legitimately attach itself to various contents – landscape, people, events, eras, values. We can think of our individual and collective souls as being the psychic function that creates and contains the playing fields for the endless encounters between instinct and spirit. And because of the elusive nature of soul as a function or a content and the essential unknowability of whether there is even such a thing as a collective soul, our topic begs to find a hook in a specific time and place.

Such a hook presented itself to me in 2004, when I was asked to moderate a conference on the theme of "The Soul of America" at the San Francisco C. G. Jung Institute. The topic was as overwhelming to me then as it is now. At the time, a deep divide in the American political psyche took on simplistic but potent symbolic form in the image of "red" and "blue" states. It was natural for the conference's topic of "The Soul of America" to veer toward a discussion of "the political fight for the soul of America."

As a Northern Californian for the past thirty-five years, with deep roots in both the Midwest and the East Coast, I chafe at the one-sidedness of most characterizations of members of one political, religious, ethnic, racial, or regional group by another. Living in a liberal region with progressive politics, I did not want to get up and proclaim that the Democrats had an inside track on the "real" soul of America or that Bush was an "idiot." Both were too easy, because those were the opinions of almost everyone in the audience, or, for that matter, of almost everyone I know. The fact is that no one group in the United States has an exclusive claim on either the "soul of America" or on being "idiots," even though one side will usually claim soul for itself and idiocy for its rival. (In the political rhetoric of the last few decades, the right has been most effective at staking out "the soul of America" for itself and far less stupid than most on the left have claimed.)

It is very easy to project soul into politics and politics into soul. Indeed, I believe it is the first task of an inquiry such as this one to try to differentiate soul from politics. This differentiation begins with the acknowledgment that soul and politics get mixed up with each other all the time in the collective psyche and in the intermingling of myth, politics, and psyche in our cultural unconscious.[2] With the goal of differentiation in mind, the first part of this chapter will address the topic of "The Soul of America," and the second part will address "Politics and the Soul of America."

Part one: what is the soul of America?

George Seferis's poem "Argonauts" tells us that to know our soul we must look in the mirror at both the stranger and enemy.[3] I believe that each of us discovers different bits and pieces of "the soul of America" as the personal journeys of our individual lives interface with the unfolding story of our nation's soul journey. When we inquire about the soul of America, I think we need to keep in mind that we are talking about a living interface between the experience of our individual souls and that of the national soul. And if looking into the depths of our personal souls often reveals mysteries, ambiguities, and contradictions, how much more complex is it to reflect on the nature of our American soul? We should begin this inquiry with the recognition that we discover the soul of America only as we discover the story of our own souls. If the Hindus speak of *Atman* and *Brahman*, perhaps we should think about an intermediary zone and speak of the individual soul and the group soul.

Let me give you a brief example that illustrates the importance of this semipermeable membrane, or interface, between personal soul and collective soul. John Perry, a well-known Jungian analyst of an earlier generation, once told me the story of his meeting, as a young man, with Jung in 1936. On one of his journeys to the United States, Jung had visited the house of John Perry's father in Providence, Rhode Island. Perry's father served there as a bishop in the Episcopal Church. Conversation with Jung at the Perry house touched on the Native American Indian's role in the story of America and the need for "modern man" to connect with the "archaic man" inside. Jung expressed his opinion that, to connect with the soul of America, one needed to connect with the American Indian. That night, a young John Perry dreamt that *he was standing by the fireplace in the living room with his hand on the mantelpiece. A bare-chested American Indian appeared in the fireplace and threw a tomahawk directly at him. In a startled response, Perry managed to catch the tomahawk in his hands.*[4] One way to think about this dream is to say that the soul of John Perry was introduced to the soul of America in his meeting with a Native American.

Not all of us have such extraordinary meetings between our individual soul and the soul of our country, but each of us is certainly startled when some aspect of America's soul appears to us in our own psychic house. In this context of the encounter of personal soul with national soul, I want to relate a story of my own unexpected personal soul meeting with a part of our nation's soul.

In July 2004, just a few months before the national elections later that fall, I traveled with my family from San Francisco to Alton, Illinois. This journey helped give me an inkling of how to speak about what the phrase "soul of America" evokes in me without falling into the easy trap – at a time of presidential elections – of identifying soul with one political group or another. It is no accident that my own musings about "the American soul" began with a personal physical journey halfway across the country, since so much of what we think of as "the soul of America" is embedded in journey – whether it be from a foreign land to the United States, or the journey from East to West to open the continent, or from West to East in search of our roots. The "journey" is at the heart of the "soul of America," and my journey to the Midwest in July 2004 was no exception.

Alton sits on the bluffs of the Mississippi River, just below where the Mississippi and Missouri rivers come together (see Figure 1.1). It is a proud old river town that celebrates its history of having been a safe haven for abolitionists in the pre–Civil War era, as well as having been the site of the famous Lincoln–Douglas debates. I had traveled to Alton with my wife and children in order to bring home the ashes of my mother-in-law, Agnes, who had died in the San Francisco Bay Area earlier in the spring. Alton was the home of Agnes's ancestors, her childhood home, and the home where she had raised her own family. Such homecomings remind us that the soul connects the material and the spiritual realms, just as the Mississippi River connects North and South, East and West in the heart of the country.

Figure 1.1 A view of Alton, Illinois, across the Mississippi

(https://aras.org/vision-folly-american-soul)

If you grow up in the Midwest, as I did, the Mississippi River reflects the soul of the country. The river's journey is the soul's journey, as Huck Finn and Tom Sawyer taught us in our youth. The grandeur of the river and the fertile surrounding valleys make it a real, symbolic, and spiritual heartland all at the same time – a flowing source of vast generosity and security. It is not an exaggeration to compare the coming together of the Missouri and Mississippi with the confluence of other great rivers of the world, such as the Tigris and Euphrates. Proud civilizations flourish in the fertile valleys and lowlands at the confluence of great rivers, and we were returning Agnes to the generous source of her origins, where her personal soul might join the American soul in its return to the origin of all souls.

Figure 1.2 The cemetery in Alton, Illinois

(https://aras.org/vision-folly-american-soul)

On July 3, 2004, having carried Agnes's ashes halfway across the country to her homeland beside the river, we traveled to the Alton Cemetery for a memorial service to honor this profoundly kind and decent woman. Agnes was widely known as "Saint Agnes" because she was like the river – vast in her giving and compassion, both to her family and friends in her personal life and to her patients in her professional life as a nurse. From the photo I took that day in the sublime cemetery

(Figure 1.2), you can see why I began to get fleeting recollections and intimations of Walt Whitman's *Leaves of Grass* as we placed Agnes's ashes in the grave next to her husband's. The cemetery's green canopy of trees and carpet of grass were both a soothing balm and a clear call to my soul, which felt deeply linked to the soul of my mother-in-law and, as Walt Whitman put it, the souls of "black folks . . . White, Kanuck, Tuckhoe, Congressman." I felt my soul resonating to the soul of the river and the soul of the town and the soul of my mother-in-law, all participating in the uniquely Midwestern incarnation of the American soul. Here is how Whitman wrote about leaves of grass, the death of old and young alike, and the meeting of individual soul and the American soul in his poem "Song of Myself":

1
I celebrate myself, and sing myself,
And what I assume you shall assume,
For every atom belonging to me as good belongs to you.

I loafe and invite my soul,
I lean and loafe at my ease observing a spear of summer grass.

My tongue, every atom of my blood, form'd from this soil, this air,
Born here of parents born here from parents the same, and their
     parents the same,
. . .

6
A child said *What is the grass?* fetching it to me with full hands;
How could I answer the child? I do not know what it is any more
     than he.

I guess it must be the flag of my disposition, out of hopeful green stuff
     woven.

Or I guess it is the handkerchief of the Lord,

A scented gift and remembrancer designedly dropt,
Bearing the owner's name someway in the corners, that we may see
     and remark, and say
Whose?

Or I guess the grass is itself a child, the produced babe of the
    vegetation.

Or I guess it is a uniform hieroglyphic,
And it means, Sprouting alike in broad zones and narrow zones,
Growing among black folks as among white,
Kanuck, Tuckahoe, Congressman, Cuff, I give them the same,
    I receive them the same.

And now it seems to me the beautiful uncut hair of graves.

Tenderly will I use you curling grass,
It may be you transpire from the breasts of young men,
It may be if I had known them I would have loved them,
It may be you are from old people, or from offspring taken soon out of
    their mothers' laps,
And here you are the mothers' laps.

This grass is very dark to be from the white heads of old mothers,
Darker than the colorless beards of old men,
Dark to come from under the faint red roofs of mouths.

O I perceive after all so many uttering tongues,
And I perceive they do not come from the roofs of mouths for
    nothing.

I wish I could translate the hints about the dead young men and
    women,
And the hints about old men and mothers, and the offspring taken
    soon out of their laps.

What do you think has become of the young and old men?
And what do you think has become of the women and children?

They are alive and well somewhere,
The smallest sprout shows there is really no death,
And if ever there was it led forward life, and does not wait at the end
    to arrest it,
And ceas'd the moment life appear'd.

All goes onward and outward, nothing collapses,
And to die is different from what any one supposed, and luckier.

. . .

31

I believe a leaf of grass is no less than the journey-work of the stars.[5]

In Section 21 of "Song of Myself," Whitman proclaims himself the bard of the American soul when he writes: "I am the poet of the Body and I am the poet of the Soul."[6] He is writing of the Body and the Soul of America, which he likens to a blade of grass whose very existence mirrors the "journey-work of the stars" in its immortality. At Agnes's service, "a blade of grass" allowed me to participate for a moment in the immortality of her soul and the American soul.

On July 4, the day following Agnes's memorial service, my family went down to the Mississippi River to join in the holiday festivities. We were at peace with ourselves and open to participating in the celebration of our nation's birth in the knowledge that we had truly accomplished the purpose of our ritual journey home. If you have not celebrated the Fourth of July by the banks of the Mississippi, I urge you to do so before you become a leaf of grass. Quite unexpectedly, there I discovered another forgotten part of Whitman's "Song of Myself" whispering to my soul as I wandered among the day's celebrants – adults guzzling beer and listening to rock 'n' roll music as the children danced and played and jumped up and down by the river's edge.

32

I think I could turn and live with animals, they are so placid and
    self-contain'd,
I stand and look at them long and long.

They do not sweat and whine about their condition,
They do not lie awake in the dark and weep for their sins,
They do not make me sick discussing their duty to God,
Not one is dissatisfied, not one is demented with the mania of owning
    things,
Not one kneels to another, nor to his kind that lived thousands of
    years ago,
Not one is respectable or unhappy over the whole earth.
. . .

52

The spotted hawk swoops by and accuses me, he complains of my gab
    and my loitering.

I too am not a bit tamed, I too am untranslatable,
I sound my barbaric yawp over the roofs of the world.[7]

Figure 1.3 Biker couple at the Fourth of July celebrations in Alton, Illinois
(https://aras.org/vision-folly-american-soul)

Figure 1.3 is an image from that celebration that got me musing about the meaning of the "Barbaric Yawp." You might find yourself wondering about my choice of this image and may find it repulsive, vulgar, or simply of little relevance to this journal's noble topic of "Politics and the American Soul." But, on this particular Fourth of July – the day after the moving memorial service for Agnes – I was fascinated by this couple as I secretly circled around behind them in an effort to capture the image of what struck me at once as so "other" and as so "barbaric." In their unabashed celebration of their own animal force, this couple evoked some primitive connection in my psyche to Whitman's "barbaric yawp."

> I too am not a bit tamed, I too am untranslatable,
> I sound my barbaric yawp over the roofs of the world.[8]

What is a "barbaric yawp"? Why did the quintessential poet of the American soul, Walt Whitman, link the "barbaric yawp" to the American soul? There are two parts to Whitman's phrase, a phrase that now brings up some 110,000 "hits" on a Google Internet search. *Barbaric* means "without civilizing influences, uncivilized, primitive" and a *yawp* is a "loud, harsh cry." Neither *barbaric* nor *yawp* suggests a civilized approach to things. Taken together, they signify a primitive enthusiasm in the form of a nonverbal cry from the essential nature of a living being. In Whitman's imagination, the essence of the American soul is neither civilized nor verbal. The "barbaric yawp" is the fierce "voice" of a soul that is essentially unrestrained and exulting in its self-expression.

One senses in my photograph of the Fourth of July biker couple an animal force that does not concern itself with – or simply flouts – more conventional norms. Adding this image to the thought that George W. Bush's Texas swagger and his inarticulate utterances are heard by many in the United States as some sort of cry from our country's "body and soul," one has to accept the fact that they are as much a part of the American soul and its "barbaric yawp" as our more progressive sensibilities. Linking George Bush and this photograph to the "barbaric yawp" is intended to be simultaneously ironic and absolutely serious. Who are we to know what or who contains the "barbaric yawp"? Who has a legitimate claim on the American soul? Again, what is the American soul?

Steven Herrmann, a Jungian with a deep scholarly interest in Whitman, wrote to me: "Whitman's 'yawp' is a *conscious* cry from the Soul of

America to make the barbarian in American political democracy conscious! The 'barbaric yawp' is Whitman's call from the depths of the American Soul to awaken the possibility of hope in a brighter future for American democracy." Herrmann went on to say:

> The aim of Whitman's "barbaric yawp" was to sound a new heroic message of "Happiness," Hope, and "Nativity" over the roofs of the world, to sound a primal cry which must remain essentially "unsaid" because it rests at the core of the American soul and cannot be found in "any dictionary, utterance, symbol" (*Leaves*, Section #50). The "barbaric yawp" is a metaphorical utterance for something "untranslatable," a primal cry from the depths of the American Soul for the emergence of man as a spiritual human being in whom the aims of liberty and equality have been fully realized and in whom the opposites of love and violence, friendship and war, have been unified at a higher political field of order than anything we have formerly seen in America. His "yawp" is an affect state, a spiritual cry of "Joy" and "Happiness" prior to the emergence of language.[9]

At this point, the reader may be wondering how it is possible to reconcile what might appear to be two very different aspects of the "barbaric yawp" that I have presented. How can the image of "Biker Dick" be part of the same "barbaric yawp" that sounds "a primal cry from the depths of the American Soul for the emergence of man as a spiritual being"? But, as Stephen Herrmann aptly points out,

> Whitman's image of man's emergence as a spiritual being refers to a person that can realize his earthly existence within the context of his total life pattern, including his depths of erotic passion. Whitman's barbarian is both a spiritual and a sexual being. He is not split inside, but whole and conscious of his full instinctive nature and lives it out according to the preference of his Soul.[10]

In contemporary America, Whitman's "barbaric yawp" is as inclusive of the violence found in the television show *The Sopranos* as it is of the unitary vision of Martin Luther King, Jr.'s "I Have a Dream." This suggests expanding our national imagination to embrace the American soul's "barbaric yawp" as both vulgar and compassionate at the same time. It was the genius of Whitman to see in the "barbaric yawp" of the American soul the capacity for an interconnected transcendent unity. This section on the Soul of America would not be complete without mentioning one final example of how glimpses of the American soul come through individual encounters that open up a window or interface between the individual soul and the larger collective soul of the group. In her preface to *Beloved*, Toni Morrison tells us that as she was gestating a novel on slavery, freedom, and the black experience, she met her main character in the following way:

> I sat on the porch, rocking in a swing, looking at giant stones piled up to take the river's occasional fist. Above the stones is a path through the lawn, but interrupted by an ironwood gazebo situated under a cluster of trees and in deep shade.
>
> She walked out of the water, climbed the rocks, and leaned against the gazebo. Nice hat.
>
> So she [Beloved] was there from the beginning, and except for me, everybody (the characters) knew it – a sentence that later became "The women in the house knew it." The figure most central to the story would have to be her, the murdered, not the murderer, the one who lost everything and had no say in any of it.[11]

Like Perry's American Indian with the tomahawk, this is a soul figure that appears out of nowhere or, as Jungians might say, "out of the unconscious" – personal, cultural, and collective. She emerges out of the water and presents herself to Toni Morrison, who is trying to figure how to create a fiction based on the true story of "Margaret Garner, a young mother who, having escaped slavery, was arrested for killing one of her children (and trying to kill the others) rather than let them be returned to the owner's plantation."[12]

The soul figure with the "nice hat" who greets Toni Morrison becomes the central character in her novel *Beloved*. Beloved is the soul of a murdered innocent, which becomes a conduit for the voices of all the other black people who perished in slavery and its aftermath. These collective voices are as deep a part of the American soul as John Perry's American Indian or Walt Whitman's barbaric yawp. Her novel roars with the sound of the white race's collective projection onto black people. Beloved becomes the spokesperson for a part of our American soul that is as much with us today as when Margaret Garner murdered her baby girl rather than return her to slavery.

Like any other soul, the American soul seeks incarnation in a specific place, at a specific time, in a specific event, and even in a specific person or groups of people. This specificity of incarnation loves location and the right person or group at the right moment. This very specificity means that many places and times in American history can claim some piece of the American soul as their own. At the same time, the American soul should not be thought of as bound to any particular person or group, any special place on the continent, or any unique time in our nation's history. As a whole, the American soul is much broader than its particularity and specificity, reaching as far back as the American Indians' migration across the Bering Strait and as far forward as one can imagine hearing Whitman's "barbaric yawp."

Part two: how does the American soul express itself in politics?

In the second section of this chapter, I want to add "politics" to the already fermenting "soul-of-America" brew that I have been stirring. The first ingredient for the political part of this American-soul concoction that comes to mind is a strangely beautiful book by Doris Lessing, *Briefing for a Descent into Hell*.[13] The central part of the novel takes its lead from the Platonic myth that this world is only a veiled shadow of the world of ideal forms. Indeed, the main character, Charles Watkins, leads us on a science-fiction journey of his inner world, in which he discovers that each individual soul is briefed before its descent to earth and its human incarnation through birth on Earth. Earth itself is described as a "poisonous hell" for which the soul needs to be prepared. This is the "briefing" of the soul, just as birth as a human is the "descent."

For many readers of this journal, the inner world is primary, and participation in the politics of the earthly realm is, in fact, a "poisonous hell." Many Jungians prefer to avoid politics altogether in favor of other, "deeper" soul work. We all know something about the soul's disillusionment when it participates in the everyday politics of institutional life – be it in the Jungian community or national presidential elections. In my own personal experience, I came away from intense engagement in Senator Bill Bradley's 2000 campaign for the Democratic Party's nomination for president feeling burned by the "poisonous hell" of earthly politics. Out of that experience (which I am sure is matched by many similar experiences among this book's readers in the political arena) I would like to share some reflections on how I am currently thinking about the relationship between politics and the American soul.

First, I don't think that the soul of America is located in identification with one party or the other. Neither party possesses the soul of America. Presumably, the soul of a right-wing fundamentalist is as engaged with the journey of the American soul as is the soul of a progressive liberal. Nor do I think the soul of America is located in one specific issue or another, whether it be abortion, immigration, discrimination based on race or other differences, gay marriage, the environment, the war in Iraq, or a host of other compelling issues.

Usually, a discussion of politics focuses on the rough and tumble of political struggle, 95 percent of which is about how to gain and exercise power. But in this meditation I am going to turn the traditional discussion of politics as it relates to power a bit upside down and focus not on Machiavelli but on some basic, recurring collective psychological themes and tensions that have coursed through our political history. These recurring themes embody deep-seated conflicts in our nation's psyche, in which neither side of the ambivalences and tensions has exclusive claim on meaning or correctness. Both sides have legitimate claim to soul.

The psychological form in which these recurring conflicts take shape over generations is what I have been exploring in the concept of "cultural complexes."[14] Each culture has its own version of how to work out basic human tensions and conflicts. The uniqueness of a culture's way of experiencing these basic human problems becomes embodied in its cultural complexes, which then play themselves out in political life. Sunnis and Shi'ites don't have the same way of dealing with their problems as Midwesterners or Southerners.

In speaking about individual complexes as revealed by the Word Association Test, Jung wrote: "Our destinies are as a rule the outcome of our psychological tendencies."[15] Another way of saying this is that our personal complexes are the hand that Fate has dealt us. How we play the hand that Fate has dealt us, or what we do with our personal complexes, determines who we become as individuals. Jung put it rather bluntly: "We all have complexes; it is a highly banal and uninteresting fact. . . . It is only interesting to know what people do with their complexes; that is the practical question which matters."[16] I believe that the same is true of our cultural complexes. What we do with our cultural complexes determines not only who we become as a people, but also the destiny of the American soul. A good deal of our working out (or not working out) of our cultural complexes occurs in the political arena.

Cultural complexes, underpinned by archetypal patterns, form the core of those highly charged struggles that have defined who we are as an American people throughout our national history. Such cultural complexes accrue a memory of their own, a point of view of their own, and a tendency to collect new experiences in contemporary life that validate their unchanging point of view. Cultural complexes also tend to fire off autonomously and with deep emotion when an event triggers them. We know that a cultural complex may well be on the scene when there is a highly aroused emotional reaction to current events. Emotional reactivity of the collective psyche is the calling card of a cultural complex.

For instance, our more than three-hundred-year conflict around race, as mirrored in the clamoring voices of Morrison's *Beloved* is an example of an entrenched cultural complex that is always ready to detonate in the psyches of white and black people. Don Imus, the well-known radio celebrity, has made a successful career out of intentionally stepping on the landmines of cultural complexes in his toying with the stereotyping of many racial and ethnic groups. But no one individual or group is immune from the destruction of self and/or of others that can come with detonating a cultural complex, as even Imus discovered in the national outrage that came on the heels of his racial slurs about black women basketball players from Rutgers University. My thesis, then, is that the American soul is embedded in our various cultural complexes. Furthermore, our cultural complexes are what give political life its dynamism and its content. Both the energy and the issues of political debate spring from the autonomous, highly charged emotional material of our core cultural complexes. Political life is the natural social arena in which cultural complexes play themselves out. We forge the American soul in our struggle with our cultural complexes. In the political arena, cultural complexes seem mostly to generate heat, division, hatred; they are inflammatory and polarizing; they usually end in a stalemate without any resolution, only to recur in the next election or the next generation; sometimes they are ignored or kept unconscious for decades; and occasionally they can be worked out slowly in engagement, compromise, reconciliation, and healing after generations of recurring battle. In short, they behave like complexes.

We might now reframe the question about the relationship of politics to the American soul as follows: "What are we doing with our cultural complexes in political life?" Or perhaps the question may be better phrased: "What are our cultural complexes doing with us in our political life?" In order to explore those questions, we need to ask: "What are our primary cultural complexes?" As a way of answering these questions, I would like to offer a list of themes or "relationships" around which cultural complexes have formed in the American psyche over the course of our nation's history.

As I briefly consider each of these "relationships," I will refer to "soul-making" and whether it appears to be happening around specific cultural complexes. I imagine soul-making as occurring when there is a legitimate claim for something of deepest human value on both sides of a conflict that has come alive in the collective psyche and has been engaged in the political arena. I hope that the reader will keep in mind that the seven American cultural complexes that I outline here interweave with one another in a tangled skein and are by no means as clear or as simple as I sketch them.

1. Our relationship to money/commerce/consumer goods

a. Core attitude of cultural complex

One of the highest values in American society has been the accumulation of personal wealth and material goods, often at the expense of or in disregard for the common good. This complex emphasizes individual achievement in the material world. On the positive side of this complex is the promised opportunity for every person to maximize his or her material well-being. The negative side of this cultural complex emphasizes our collective and individual right to eat the world, own the world, amass personal wealth, and continuously increase the "gross national product." In the name of participating in the American Dream, consumerism has become almost synonymous with the highest good.[17]

b. Specific current political issue: campaign finance reform

In an attempt to curb the equation of material wealth with the common good, recent efforts have been made to introduce campaign finance reform as a way of equalizing the role of money in a democratic society. These attempts have been "dead on arrival" and have been undermined by both parties. On this issue, there is no "soul-making" occurring in either major political party. There is little meaningful engagement in the political arena with the overemphasis on money and consumerism in our civic life and in our political life. We are soul-dead regarding active, conscious engagement with this cultural complex. Our collective psyche is consumed by its consumerism. (Al-Qaeda was very conscious of this when it attacked the World Trade Center.)

2. Our relationship to the natural environment

a. Core attitude of cultural complex

Historically, we have been a country of vast and seemingly unlimited natural resources. This has fostered a cultural complex based on the belief that this blessing entitles us to everything we want and that we own everything in the natural world. A growing number of people have come to understand that "stewardship" is the responsibility that goes along with the privilege of vast but dwindling natural resources.

b. Specific current political issues

There are a host of ongoing political debates related to the environment suggesting that soul-making is going on with regard to this cultural complex.

These include policy conflicts about global warming, clean air and water, the limitation of natural resources, and the desire to use those limited resources wisely.

3. Our relationship to the human community, including family life, social life, and the life cycle from conception to death

a. Core attitude of cultural complex

This country was built on a belief in the inalienable rights and freedoms of the individual as much as it was built on utopian communalism. A core American cultural complex spins out of the unending dynamic tension between the myth of the self-sufficient individual in opposition to the welfare of the community as a whole and the reality of the community's responsibility to the individual. The good of the whole and all its members is endlessly challenged by the rights of the individual.

b. Specific current political issues

This cultural complex is ubiquitous in our political debates and makes itself known in all sorts of issues that range from the right to bear arms and taxation to national healthcare policy and how to fund pensions and Social Security. Again, national soul-making appears to be going on in the engagement of this cultural complex. The debate over the rights and responsibilities of the individual in relationship to the needs of the collective and its responsibilities to all its members engages citizens across the political spectrum.

4. Our relationship to the spiritual realm

a. Core attitude of cultural complex

Our Puritan heritage launched our country both in dissent and in a tradition of strict belief in moralistic behavior. The belief that America has a special relationship to God fuels our sense of national entitlement, which is matched only by our strong tradition of religious dissent, which drives our national skepticism about privileged authority, divine or otherwise. Out of these twin foundational attitudes grew our tradition of separation of church and state. Inclusive pluralism and dogmatic fundamentalism are the vying poles of a uniquely American cultural complex that is the psychological inheritance of our religious traditions. As in many other countries, the archetypal split between good and evil in our collective psyche projects itself onto many political issues, from the clash over abortion to the debate about the war in Iraq.

b. Specific current political issue: abortion

Perhaps about as much soul-making has been going on around this issue as around any in recent political history. Although the issue has generated murderous heat, it has also raised fundamental questions about the nature of soul and life, which, to my mind, are part of any healthy debate in society. The clash of religious fundamentalism with the rights of a woman to make choices about her own body in a society that values the separation of church and state cuts across so many of our cultural complexes that I think it forces everyone to sort out what he or she believes on an incredibly difficult series of issues. That is soul-making. It has turned many things upside down in our society. For instance, conservatives most often align themselves with the rights of the self-sufficient individual, and progressives side with the needs of all in the community. But on the issue of abortion, progressives uphold the right to individual choice, whereas conservatives argue for a community value that applies to all.

5. Our relationship to race, ethnicity, gender – all the "others"

a. Core attitude of cultural complex

There have been two distinct poles in the American cultural complex regarding race, ethnicity, and gender. As much as in any other country in the world, inclusiveness in terms of race, ethnicity, and gender has been part of our national character and its proud "melting-pot" history. But ever since the nation's inception, the radioactive background behind the apparent embrace of diversity has been the premise that white, Anglo-Saxon, heterosexual men were destined to dominate the nation.

b. Specific current political issues: same-sex marriage, immigration

The powerful unconscious hold of the cultural complex of discrimination on the basis of sex, race, ethnicity, and age has been challenged on multiple levels simultaneously in the past several decades. Indeed, the assault on the established complex has been so thorough that the new cultural complex replacing it – "political correctness" – has itself become the dominant persona of the collective, behind which lurks the shadow of stereotyping on the basis of differences. In a sense, white male dominance and the embracing of diversity can be thought of as two sides of the same coin of this cultural complex. But, most importantly for our discussion, soul-making in the collective psyche is occurring at unprecedented speed with regard to the active engagement of this complex, in such potent current political issues as same-sex marriage and immigration and in the fact that for the first time in American history, a black man, a woman, and a Mormon are running simultaneously for the presidential nomination.

6. Our relationship to speed, height, youth, progress, celebrity

a. Core attitude of cultural complex

As the "new land," America has always been identified with what is new – a new land with new people and new ideas, faster, higher, younger, ever progressing, ever renewing itself. The wedding of celebrity, charisma, and ingenuity are forever the hope of the American Dream and American politics. The "new land" gave substance to the belief in our nation's unique destiny, poignantly portrayed in John Gast's *American Progress* from 1872 (Figure 1.4). This wonderful illustration shows an archetypal anima figure who serves as a symbolic image of the American soul's identification with "Progress." "She" – the American soul as Progress – floats at the core of a national cultural complex of entitlement, exceptionalism, and the "American Dream."

Figure 1.4 John Gast's *American Progress* (1872)

(https://aras.org/vision-folly-american-soul)

b. Specific current political issue: stem cell research

This political debate has tremendous potential for soul-making in the collective psyche because it pits what is "God-given" against what is "new." Surely, there is soul on both sides of the debate. Our addiction to creating something new, quicker, easier, better is a source of American ingenuity and prosperity. It endlessly challenges what has existed for a long time, if not forever. For many, what has existed forever is good enough, and for some it is even God's will.

In John Gast's *American Progress*, a diaphanously and scantily clad woman representing America floats westward through the air with the "Star of Empire" on her forehead. She has left the cities of the East behind and the wide Mississippi, and still her course is westward. In her right hand, she carries a schoolbook, a testimonial to the National Enlightenment, while in her left she trails the slender wires of the telegraph, which will bind the nation together. Fleeing her approach are Indians, buffalo, wild horses, bears, and other game, all of which disappear into the storm and waves of the Pacific Coast. They flee the wondrous vision – the star "is too much for them."[18]

7. Our relationship to the world beyond our borders

a. Core attitude of cultural complex

The theme of the freedom of the individual versus the individual's responsibility to the whole is writ large in the cultural complex of our relationship to the broader world beyond American borders. In this case, our nation arrogates to itself, as a nation, the same rights as the individual, whose freedom it sees as paramount. As an "individual" nation, we place our economic and security interests for the most part above our responsibility to the global community. The tension between the freedom of the individual and the individual's responsibility to the whole in this complex joins forces with another cultural complex: our sense of entitlement, which comes from our view of ourselves as exceptional and therefore as knowing what is best for the world. These two cultural complexes get acted out in peculiar ways – we wage war in other parts of the world in the name of individual freedoms just as easily as we retreat from broader engagement in the world in the name of individualistic isolationism, which renounces responsibility to the broader whole.

b. Specific current political issues

The American-led war in Iraq is a horrific contemporary example of how a cultural complex (or more than one cultural complex) can seize the collective psyche and come alive in politics. Part of the motivation for waging this war grows out of a deep-seated American belief that affirms the unique destiny of our people as guardians of democratic principles and therefore as exceptional, blessed by God with endless opportunity, perhaps even eternal youth and immortality as a nation. The conduct of the Iraq War has revealed the flaws in a cultural complex that puts the nation's rugged individualism ahead of a sense of responsibility to and participation in the global community. The experiences of the wars in Vietnam and now Iraq have begun the slow process of challenging these core beliefs that sit at the heart of those fundamental American cultural complexes in which our fierce individualism joins forces with our sense of entitlement and exceptionalism. As the deflation of bankrupt policies settles into the collective psyche, one hopes that this terrible misadventure has had its soul-making impact on the body politic.

Conclusion

In each of the broad areas that I have characterized as cultural complexes, a set of specific issues take center stage at any given time in the political life of our country. In the great crucible of politics, where our core cultural complexes enter the political life of the nation, the American soul gets forged and crucified – made, remade, unmade, made again – over and over. These autonomous psychological clusters of memory, affect, and repetitive historical behavior seize our collective psyche in an endless round of racial strife, economic striving, gender warfare, and unending worship of technology, progress, speed, height, information, youth, innocence, moral simplicity, heroic achievement, and insatiable consumerism, all of which have addicted the entire nation – Democrats, Republicans, independents, and the uncommitted alike. It is the "barbaric yawp" of the American soul embodied in political life.

Signs of soul life can clearly be detected in the growing conflict around our relationship to the natural environment. Such signs can also be detected in the intensifying struggles and rapidly changing collective attitudes to race, gender, and sexual identity. In these particular cultural complexes, the American soul seems to be transforming itself through highly engaged political activity. On the other hand, our country is so addicted to money, to speed, to youth, to consumerism, and to progress that our collective soul seems lost or invisible in our possession by these complexes. Our national politics regarding these possessions seems hopelessly unengaged and unconscious. Lively debate on the current political issues generated by these underlying cultural complexes that course through our history like an underground river are essential to the continuing growth of our collective psyche and our individual souls as well.

The politics of the day that challenge our more entrenched cultural complexes are met with the same kind of fierce resistance from groups that an analyst encounters when asking a patient to take on or confront a personal complex – or that the ego faces when it encounters the unconscious resistance of an entrenched complex, which does its best to keep from being known or made conscious. Frankly, I was surprised, in taking this most approximate inventory of our cultural complexes, that I reached the conclusion that soul-making activity is taking place in so many areas of our political life. When I began writing this chapter, I would have said that there was little happening in our political life that suggested soul. Of course, many readers may disagree with my conclusions.

Many in our country would prefer that the sound of our national soul be less of a yawp and closer to the "Om" of Hinduism. "Om" evokes compassion, peace, reverence, unity. To make a bad pun, "Om" is a far cry from Whitman's primal "barbaric yawp." But the reality is that the sound of the American soul is messier than "Om," and when the barbaric yawp sounds its discordant note in politics, it rarely is unifying or resonant of deep compassion. Rather, at its best, it vibrates with dynamism, energy, and the promise of renewal. Perhaps we should be most afraid of the time in our country when the mix of politics and soul has left us so deadened by disillusionment and distrust that we are unable even to hear the barbaric yawp.

Notes

1 Thomas Singer, "A Personal Meditation on Politics and the American Soul," *Politics and the American Soul* 78 (2007), was originally published in 2007 in *Spring Journal*.
2 Thomas Singer, ed., *The Vision Thing: Myth, Politics and Psyche in the World* (London and New York: Routledge, 2000).
3 George Seferis, "Argonauts," in *Collected Poems: 1924–1955*, ed., trans. and intro. Edmund Keeley and Philip Sherrard (Princeton: Princeton University Press, 1967), 9.
4 Personal communication with John Perry.
5 Walt Whitman, "Song of Myself," in *Leaves of Grass*, Project Gutenberg, www.gutenberg.org/ebooks/1322.
6 Ibid.
7 Ibid., my italics.
8 Ibid.
9 Personal communication with Steven Herrmann.
10 Ibid.
11 Toni Morrison, *Beloved* (New York: Vintage Books, 1987), xviii. Excerpt(s) from BELOVED by Toni Morrison, copyright © 1987 by Toni Morrison. Used by permission of Alfred A. Knopf, an imprint of the Knopf Doubleday Publishing Group, a division of Penguin Random House LLC. All rights reserved.
12 Ibid., xvii.
13 Doris Lessing, *Briefing for a Descent into Hell* (London: Vintage Books, 1981).
14 See Thomas Singer, "The Cultural Complex and Archetypal Defenses of the Collective Spirit: Baby Zeus, Elian Gonzales, Constantine's Sword, and Other Holy Wars," *The San Francisco Library Journal* 20, no. 4 (2002): 4–28; Thomas Singer, "Cultural Complexes and Archetypal Defenses of the Group Spirit," in *Terror, Violence and the Impulse to Destroy*, ed. John Beebe (Zürich: Daimon Verlag, 2003), 191–209; Thomas Singer and Samuel L. Kimbles, eds., *The Cultural Complex: Contemporary Jungian Perspectives on Psyche and Society* (London and New York: Routledge, 2004).
15 C. G. Jung, *The Collected Works of C. G. Jung, vol. 4, Freud and Psychoanalysis* (Princeton: Princeton University Press, 1961), 309.

16 C. G. Jung, "The Tavistock Lectures, Lecture 3," in *Analytical Psychology: Its Theory and Practice* (New York: Vintage Books, 1968), 94.

17 Jack Beatty, *Age of Betrayal: The Triumph of Money in America, 1865–1900* (New York: Alfred Knopf, 2007).

18 Adapted from a contemporary description of Gast's painting, written by George Crofutt, who distributed his engraving of it widely. Source: www.csubak. edu/~gsantos/img0061.html.

2 The meshugana complex
Notes from a big galoot galut

From *Jung Journal: Culture & Psyche*, 2012.[1]

In 2011, the C. G. Jung Institute of San Francisco hosted a conference on "Jung and Judaism: Paradoxical Affinities." The conference was intended to address the close connections between Jung and Judaism that were in danger of being swept away by an exclusive focus on the theme of Jung and anti-Semitism. Jung Journal published the papers given at the conference in 2012. The subtitle of this paper, "Notes from a Big Galoot Galut," is a play on words about myself as a "galoot/ galut." A galoot is an awkward or foolish person, and a galut refers to a Jew in exile. The theme of the "galut" emerged several times in the conference where it was used somewhat pejoratively to refer to those Jews who are not only physically in exile, but also inwardly in exile from a relationship to their living faith and God.

The title for this chapter, "The Meshugana Complex," came to me late one night. By the next morning, I had already begun to doubt myself, as *meshugana* is a Yiddish word that means "crazy or crazy person." My concern was that the title might suggest an anti-Semitic bias in my chapter by characterizing the Jung/Jewish issue as a uniquely Jewish problem, such as a Jewish craziness of being overly sensitive to anti-Semitic undercurrents. The truth is that I didn't quite know what I meant by *meshugana complex* when it popped into my mind, but I hope that by the end of this chapter we will discover together why the title might actually make sense.

The topic of Jung and the Jewish connection first surfaces in Jung's 1913 confrontation with his own unconscious Red One, who essentially tells Jung in *The Red Book* that he is a joyless, humorless anti-Semite.[2] In many ways, Jung's unconscious anticipated his critics who have been saying essentially the same thing for almost one hundred years now. This long-standing thorn in the Jung/Jewish connection is just a tiny blip on the historical screen of the much older story of Christian/Jewish conflict that is documented so beautifully in James Carroll's *Constantine's Sword*.[3] The subtitle of this paper – "Paradoxical Affinities" – is taken from the title of the 2011 "Jung and Judaism" conference and adds a certain "meshugana" seasoning to the stew that has been brewing for a hundred years, in the relationship between Jung and Jewishness, and for almost two thousand years, in the relationship between Christians and Jews.

I find the phrase "paradoxical affinities" elegant and evocative. It should come as no surprise that the phrase was created by the organizer of the conference: Baruch Gould, a Jew.[4] Throughout history, Jews have specialized in "paradoxical affinities." In my mind, an essential aspect of the dialectic that is contained within the idea of a "paradoxical affinity" is the existential angst of being caught between different groups and not centered in one's own home. That has been the essence of Jews living in exile since the destruction of the Temple. At a minimum, being Jewish and being Jungian speaks of belonging to two distinct tribes – one very old and the other very new.

Given its complicated and tortuous history, the wonderful and monstrous topic of the "paradoxical affinities" between Jung and the Jewish connection begs for context. The fact is that the personal, family, and cultural histories of everyone who attended the conference (Jewish and non-Jewish) have meaningful overlaps, but I also know that there are very significant differences among us that give us each a different "take" on this topic. For instance, being a Jew with origins on the East Coast is quite different from being a Jew from the South, the Midwest, or the Far West – just as being a Jew from Germany or Eastern Europe or Iran or Jerusalem is different. We may all share many things, including an interest in the "paradoxical affinities" of Jung and the Jewish connection, but we are not all the same, and I think we would be making a big mistake if we take either being Jewish or Jungian to be *one* thing. Just as it would be a mistake to think all Jews share a common experience, it would also a mistake to think that Jung was one thing to himself or to all the Jews and non-Jews. We can't describe Jung and the Jewish connection without knowing our own relationship to Jewishness and without knowing who we think Jung was.

I do know that my story is different from that of many of my dear Jewish colleagues – and sometimes I feel guilty that I am not Jewish enough and don't deserve to be writing about this topic. One of my Jewish colleagues who knows me well laughed when I told her my title and quipped, "I didn't know you even knew the word 'meshugana.'" On the other hand, I don't feel guilty that I'm not Jungian enough – but maybe that's the difference between being Jewish and being Jungian. I think Jews can easily out-guilt Jungians and just about everyone else – except perhaps the Catholics, which is why Catholics and Jews often understand one another so well.

I would like to start by grounding my remarks in the "particular" of my experience of Jung and Jewishness and gradually move to the more universal, because I get very uncomfortable with generalizing or "archetypalizing" when the uniqueness of person, place, and time is not first acknowledged and established.

To start with the particulars of my own reality, I was caught between two tribes at an early age. My father's family settled in St. Louis, Missouri, in the late 1840s. They were part of an early wave of German Jews who fled the social and economic turmoil of Europe. They were a particular "tribe" identified by religion, ethnicity, country of origin, and date of arrival – a tribe that was close-knit and did not mix much with other "tribes" in terms of marriage, social life, religious worship, or business affiliations. This early wave of my German Jewish immigrant ancestors has prospered in America over the past 160 years to reach a level of financial and social status that few of the early immigrants would have imagined possible.

They settled in the major cities of the United States: New York; Boston; Washington, D.C.; Cleveland; Louisville; Chicago; Cincinnati; San Francisco; St. Louis; and many other cities and towns as well. Sometimes I imagine that they were led west by Gene Wilder in the movie *Blazing Saddles*, even though I think Wilder's character started his movie journey West as an Eastern European Jew. The German Jewish tribe maintained contact by traveling from city to city and by doing business with one another; later on, their grandchildren or great-grandchildren would meet at colleges and universities around the country – in spite of a quota system that limited the number of Jews in most such places. This enclave intermarried and thrived, maintaining a very specific ethnic and class identity. As they became more assimilated, many of them moved away from their religious roots in Judaism but not from their cultural values, which placed a high premium on education, philanthropy, and humanism. As a group, the tribe of German Jews who immigrated in the 1840s was highly successful as merchants, as professionals, and in finance. They founded most of the major department store chains in the United States and such ventures as Levi Strauss in San Francisco. This group became so affluent that, by the time I was growing up, they had many summer camps for their children in states like Maine and Michigan, to which they packed away their boys and girls for eight weeks every summer.

So in the summer of 1950 – when I was eight years old – I was put on a train in St. Louis, Missouri, where my father's family had settled one hundred years earlier. My mother's family had settled in Louisville, Kentucky, where my great-grandfather founded both a Jewish hospital and a bourbon distillery before he died in 1917. I have often wished that the distillery had remained in the family. I traveled on the train for two days before we arrived halfway across the country at Camp Kennebec in Waterville, Maine. The only person I knew on this long journey was my brother, who was seven years older. He had been making the same trip for several summers.

My most vivid memory of that journey came following the second day, when the train stopped in the dead of night, in the middle of nowhere, and we were told to disembark. We were not in a station. It was very dark and there was nothing around, except a truck with a canvas top, into the back of which we were herded. I did not know where we were or what was happening. I began to cry and continued to do so pretty much without interruption for two weeks. I was so angry with my parents that I wrote them a letter, threatening never to come home again unless they sent me some chewing gum. They arranged for my older brother to come across Lake Salmon from the "Senior Camp" to visit me at the "Junior Camp," because I was inconsolable. My brother remembers me making a continuous, strange, high-pitched clicking noise in my throat. Eventually, my intense separation anxiety dissipated, and I settled into camp life, which included taking on the identity of the Micmac tribe, a part of the greater Abenaki Nation that comprised the original Native American inhabitants of Central Maine. Not surprisingly, I ended up thriving for the next eight summers in this boy's dreamland of lakes, rivers, mountains, and endless competitive sports. It seems a bit ironic now, though, to think that young Jewish boys, mostly from ancestors who emigrated from Germany, were being sent off to Maine just after the end of World War II to behave as if they were American Indians – swimming, canoeing, and hiking. And, in my case – perhaps as a harbinger of my life to come – I became the medicine man, whose role it was to chant at the great tribal campfires: "Ay Oon Koony As Nay, Noon Way."

What's even stranger is that getting off the train that first night in the state of Maine in 1950 became a kind of "screen memory" that equated itself in my mind over time with what we might now label a "cultural unconscious identification" with my German Jewish ancestors – with my being shipped off to Auschwitz. Somewhere between the personal and cultural levels of the unconscious in my psyche, I made the equation between the intense suffering of separation from my family with the suffering of the Jews in Germany. The reality is that I was the son of a privileged American Jewish family, and I was going off to learn how to swim, play tennis, and canoe – not to die in the gas chambers.

A year or so later, in 1952, at the age of ten, I left my predominantly Jewish elementary school, Glenridge, to begin a new school in St. Louis that both my father and brother had attended before me – a fine private secondary school, The St. Louis Country Day School, where we all wore coats and ties every day beginning in the fifth grade and sang "Onward

Christian Soldiers" in the school chapel on Tuesdays and Thursdays. That hymn added to my thin repertoire of the one other spiritual song that I knew and had sung every Christmas at our mostly Jewish elementary school: "Silent Night, Holy Night," a song that I still love to this day.

When I went to St. Louis Country Day School as a fifth grader, I suddenly became part of the 10 percent of the Jewish quota that was being admitted to the exclusive schools of the White Anglo-Saxon Protestant (WASP) majority – the identified social power of the era. Nobody told me about the quota, although some inborn radar figured out very quickly that there were five Jews in our class of sixty boys.

Culturally, I identified as a Jew and still do, but my religious upbringing was nonexistent, as my father had left the temple when he was ten years old in 1917. At that time, he was also attending St. Louis Country Day School. One Sunday at Temple School, his teacher told the class that they should "never trust the goy." My father protested, as he felt friendship and acceptance at his mostly Christian school. He was cited for insubordination and was sent to the office of the head of the Sunday school, where he was chided for questioning the authority of his religious teachers. He left the temple but continued to be active in Jewish and other nondenominational civic activities all his life. My mother was a proclaimed atheist by the time she was sixteen and had no interest whatsoever in religious life.

At a relatively early age, I had begun to figure out that the world was divided into different groups who did not socialize with one another or trust one another. There were separate country clubs and separate dancing schools – although I imagine that, whether Christian or Jewish, the dancing schools were equally dreadful for most boys. This separation based on ethnicity and religion wasn't just true for the Christians and Jews. The other group that I had the most contact with was the African Americans. They were the most obviously different group, and they suffered the clearest and most virulent discrimination. They were also the cooks, cleaning women, gardeners, and drivers with whom many of us in St. Louis grew up in our homes. And, many decades later, it was the black women from a local church who provided the loving day-to-day care of my failing mother, who eventually died at the age of ninety-one in the bedroom of her home of seventy years. Slavery had ended one hundred years earlier, but we were raised in such a racist, segregated society that we were unaware we were even racist.

As time went on, I became increasingly conscious of the schisms between different groups of people. I went to school aware that "Onward Christian Soldiers" was not "my" song. I came home to dinners prepared and served by black cooks, and in the summer, I went to a camp where the traditional roles of Christians and Jews were reversed; Jews were the majority and ruling class, and the few Christian boys at the camp worked in the kitchen and cleaned the Jewish boys' dishes. I returned for my final summer at Camp Kennebec as a sixteen-year-old, in the somewhat honored position of waiter in the camp dining room. This was my first real job, as it was for most of the former campers, and represented a transition from boyhood to the working world of young men. Here, too, was a stratified and segregated world: Jewish boys who had been campers worked as waiters in the dining room. Christian boys – mostly from Philadelphia, the City of Brotherly Love – worked in the kitchen. I moved back and forth between the two worlds of the dining room and that of the kitchen easily. Unlike most of the other Jewish boys at the camp, who were from East Coast cities and went to schools in predominantly Jewish neighborhoods, I came from a Midwestern city and attended a school and played sports in a world populated mostly by Christians. So, when a kitchen boy got sick and had to leave camp early in the summer, I was asked to take his place in the kitchen and "swill" garbage with the Christians, which I was perfectly comfortable doing.

As the summer wore on, I was mostly oblivious to the underlying tensions that had been festering between the two groups until the darkness of the final night, when the Christian boys – who slept in a separate cabin – attacked the Jewish boys' cabin and a nasty fight broke out. I remember chaos: a lot of shouting, a few punches, and the terrible confusion of trying to stop a violent fight that made no sense to me. Here were clearly forces beyond my understanding that I could not control and that I was not able to mediate. My very first experience of Kennebec left me somehow imagining that I had been shipped off to a concentration camp, and, in my very last experience, I found myself in the middle of a fist fight between Jews and Christians, both groups with which I identified and felt comfortable. I was at home in two worlds that harbored age-old hostilities for one another. The fact is that I loved the camp and I loved the school. Although the separation anxiety I experienced as an eight-year-old was intense, it is also a fact that my childhood was not at all traumatic by today's standards. I present these minor skirmishes of my youth simply to give you some insight into how each of us – whether our suffering has been minor or horrendous – can be sensitized to the strife between groups and how that strife, whether passed on through ancestral memory or direct experience or both, works its way into the "inner sociology" of our cultural complexes. Every Jew has a personal history of relationships to non-Jews and can recite such histories relatively easily – ones that will either reinforce the historical experience of pervasive anti-Semitism in the Western world or reveal acceptance and/ or assimilation into a non-Jewish world. Every Jew can probably place themselves on a spectrum of trust versus distrust of the non-Jewish world – especially in regard to Christians.

Where one places oneself on such a spectrum is part of that inner sociology we all construct unconsciously from an early age, which builds itself on personal and group experiences of differences and hostilities between groups that we either belonged to or didn't. Occasionally, most of us have had the experience of bridging otherwise separate groups through friendship or some other experience of getting to know someone from the "other" group.

I learned early enough that life in groups can be difficult – both in adapting to one's own "native" group and in navigating thoughtfully among different groups competing for truth, power, money, recognition, and sometimes even survival. Many of our deepest and most confusing feelings about loyalty, honor, identity, belonging, guilt, betrayal, responsibility, and common humanity get stirred up in the cauldron of the emotional life that courses through rivalrous groups – whether German and Jewish, Jungian and Freudian, Christian and Muslim, black and white, gay and straight, men and women, Jewish and Jungian, or gangs of blacks and Latinos on the streets of many cities in the United States today.

In a historical era and country where the autonomy and sanctity of the individual are part of our birthright, the belief in the unique development of the individual is taken to be the most natural course of events, which is confirmed by our political and psychological theories. We also believe this unique value of the individual to be of universal applicability. These beliefs make it hard for us to realize that, since the beginning of time, for most people around the world, their group identity is often the only and, by far, the most important identity that they have. It is also hard to believe that the idea of the immortality of the individual soul is relatively new, and for most of human history, the ongoing life of the tribe or group or city has been much more important than the quality of an individual life. Jung's idea of individuation is a drop of water in the ocean of human evolution when it comes to the much older and stronger belief that it is the existence of the tribe that matters. One of the paradoxical affinities in the relationship between Jung and Jewishness is the tension between individual development so valued in Jungian analysis and tribal belonging so essential to Jewish identity and survival. Being Jungian and Jewish incarnates the tension between these different values and is part of the paradoxical affinity that we experience – although often it seems that the values reverse, and Jungians huddle together as if they are the only tribe in the world while Jews are out in the world fighting for the rights of individuals of all groups. By the time of my adolescence, I knew that I was a member of a minority group, the Jews, although I experienced no anti-Semitism at my mostly Christian school, where I felt at home. The fact is that I really didn't have a clue about what it actually meant to be a Jew or a Christian in a religious sense. I was very much like a Christian friend of mine from camp, who told me how he used to wonder about who this "Round John Virgin" character was whom they sang about at Christmas time.

I did have a feeling for the cultural identity that went along with belonging to a Jewish family or a Christian family. But mostly I felt a vague spiritual vacuum and hungered for real knowledge about the nature of human existence. Country Day School offered a tremendous education in literature, and beginning in our freshman year of high school, we learned to read great books with a keen eye toward understanding the nature of symbols. By my senior year in high school, I was writing a thesis on Camus's work, especially *The Stranger, The Plague*, and *The Fall*. That was the beginning of my spiritual education, which led to my majoring in Religion and European Literature at Princeton University, where my senior thesis was on Nikos Kazantzakis. My hunger for a spiritual education found grounding in theology and literature. My most inspired teacher, Malcolm Diamond, was a Jew who taught "Problems of Religious Thought" with a passion that spoke of spiritual depth and vitality. By the time I graduated from college, I would describe myself as an assimilated Jew wrestling with questions about the nature of human existence that were not answered by any sense of belonging either to the Jewish or Christian faith.

The study of Kazantzakis led me to become a teaching fellow in Athens the year after graduating from college. It broke my world open in the most wonderful way and, for a time, put my questioning mind on a wholly different path that would, in time, lead me to believe that I really belonged in the Minoan civilization of ancient Greece, which existed even before the multiplicity of gods ascended Mount Olympus. This certainly solved the Jewish/Christian problem for me (later to become the Jung/Jewish "paradoxical affinities"), because there were no Christians or Jungians at that time – and the Jews were worlds away in Egypt, as this was even before the parting of the Red Sea. Perhaps there were not even "paradoxical affinities" then. Unfortunately, I was not permitted to stay in that altered state very long, as the return to first-year medical school the following year plunged me into a long, hard, deep journey that ended some seventeen years later, when I woke up to discover that I was a Jungian analyst. Becoming Jungian was the only way that I could find some resolution to being a doctor and a psychiatrist deeply interested in the relationship between spirit, psyche, and matter. Jung became the "reconciling bridge" between the worlds of spirit and matter that assaulted me with their horrors and wonders in medical school. Of some interest is the fact that I was introduced to the living reality of the Jungian tradition by a Christian in the basement of Yale Medical School in 1967. His name was Ray Walker, and his life had been radically transformed by a Jungian analysis with Esther Harding. But becoming a full-fledged Jungian between the years of 1967 and 1982 did not resolve the childhood issue of living between two tribes. The old Christian/Jewish issue of tribal belonging was deeply embedded in the Freudian and Jungian traditions of that era. Becoming a Jungian felt like a betrayal of my Jewish tribal identity. Not only was I a cultural Jew – if not a practicing Jew – but both my parents also had benefited enormously from Freudian analysis. How can a good Jewish son of parents analyzed in the Freudian tradition become a Jungian and not a Freudian? My family had often been criticized by other more Jewish families for our assimilationist behavior and aspirations to belong to a wider non-Jewish world, as symbolized by my father becoming one of the first Jewish members of a very WASPy men's business eating club – the Noon Day Club – and by our attending St. Louis Country Day School. My father firmly believed in not being separatist and renounced the isolationist exclusivity of many Jews who refused to have much to do with non-Jews. He still rejected the lesson he heard as a ten-year-old: "Never trust the goy." Bridging different groups means enduring potential criticism from both groups.

This has been as true of the bridging of Jungian and Freudian groups as it is of bridging Christian and Jewish groups. In their history, the Freudians and the Jungians have in some way been a mirror image in the realm of psychology of the age-old rivalry between Christians and Jews – although in the case of Freudians and Jungians, the Jewish Freudians had the power over the mostly Christian Jungians (just as the Jews ruled the roost over the Christians at Camp Kennebec). This was especially true between about 1950 to 1990, when this rivalry was most intense. The Freudians were in control of most major psychiatric training programs at university hospitals and medical schools. Now both groups are like first-cousin dinosaurs on the verge of extinction. But back in the days when the Titans were battling for control of the psychoanalytic world, Jungians were hardly in the battle. The primary armamentarium of the Jungians was to repeat endlessly the mantra that Freudians were "reductionists" who embraced a "mono-myth." From a Jungian perspective, both of these attributes were abhorrent. Jungians took comfort in being a misunderstood minority who had access to the real depths of human experience. Freudians would accuse Jungians of being wooly headed mystics and anti-Semites. As the dominant group, Freudians mostly just denied the existence of Jungians and pleaded "dumb" when anything Jungian was introduced. As we all know, the most annihilating anxieties are generated by those who refuse to acknowledge our existence. The Freudians used the great silent treatment, reinforced by the endless repetitions of Jung's alleged anti-Semitic, pro-Nazi proclivities.[5]

For years, I felt trapped between these warring groups, secretly believing that both groups were wrong and both groups were right – those are real "paradoxical affinities"! The war between the Freudian and Jungian groups went on in my psyche for years, as it did in the outer world as well. It wasn't until I began to think of the battle in terms of the theory of cultural complexes that something began to release inside me and I felt freer to be myself.[6] I began to realize that what the two internalized groups had to say about one another was full of distortions, misunderstandings, and projections on both sides – that both groups were in the grips of a cultural complex with regard to one another and that the internal embodiment of that complex created a very real shadow war in myself.

The concept of the cultural complex became so important to me because it helped me work through and gain a clearer psychological perspective on the deeply conflicted feelings of loyalty and betrayal that I had experienced ever since gravitating to Jung more than Freud and being as comfortable with Christians as Jews growing up. I had discovered from the mid-1960s onward that Jungians had very fixed opinions of Freudians and Freudians of Jungians. The theory of cultural complexes, with its emphasis on autonomous, repetitive patterns of thoughts and feelings that continually collect new experiences to validate their fixed, rigid understandings of ancestral and recurring trauma, allowed me to place the conflicts of the Jungians and Freudians in some perspective. Perhaps all the inner and outer turmoil between these rivalrous groups as they live in the psyches of individuals and the culture is what I mean by the "meshugana complex."

As the awareness of these inner cultural complexes grew, I began to feel some of the internal conflict dissolve. The habitual dumbness of Freudians about Jung, a kind of stubborn stupidity, the inferiority feelings of Jungians masquerading as "superiority" to those who don't really understand the depths of the psyche, the tremendous automatic hostilities, suspicions, and animosities – they all seemed less personal and less important to me, as I began to recognize them as the attitudes and feelings of the group complexes that had taken up residence within my own psyche. They seemed to separate themselves out from my identity with them as they lost their grip on my own experience of the world. Inside, it began to feel as if two large balloons filled with noxious gases had gradually deflated and began to take up less and less space in my thinking and feeling. Cultural complexes can eat us alive, particularly when they possess us unconsciously.

I believe that the world provides ample evidence for the fact that our tribal belonging can become much more essential to us than anything else, despite all the conscious emphasis we place on individuation. A significant part of the Jung/Jewish story of paradoxical affinities is one of cultural complexes in which both groups claimed to carry the real truth of the human psyche and found the other group to be terribly misguided, just plain wrong, or downright evil. To be a member of one group was to betray the other. Others may not have experienced it this way, but I did. To be a Jungian was to betray being Jewish/Freudian. Being Jewish/Freudian was to betray being Jungian.

And here is where we encounter one of the more interesting historical twists about the Jung/Jewish paradoxical affinities. Let me state it as simply as I can: Freud was Jewish. But he was not spiritual. In fact, he believed that most things spiritual were infantile wish fulfillment. Freud was an anti-religious Jew. This anti-religious attitude is one of the foundations of his psychology. Sex and aggression live in the unconscious, not spirit. Jung was Christian. And he was spiritual in an unconventional way. He believed that spirit was at the heart of human experience, and he postulated a positive life of the spirit as part of the collective unconscious. The heart of the paradoxical affinity that is most compelling to me in my reflections on Jung and the Jewish connection is that Jews in search of spirit were able to find that in Jung. They could not find it in Freud.

The reality of this assertion was confirmed in my reading of Tom Kirsch's manuscript of *The Jungians*.[7] I was startled to realize that many of Jung's most important early followers were German Jews. The list of early German Jews who followed Jung includes Adler, Kirsch, Bernhard, Neumann, Westman, Kluger, and Jaffé. Many of them were founders of Jungian Institutes around the world. Why was this? I imagined them to be like me in that they were assimilated Jews of their times who had mostly enjoyed the benefits of assimilation into their culture. But I also imagined that, like me, they had lost contact with the living reality of the spirit, which they did not find in their Judaism. So, they were attracted to Jung, not to Freud. The help that Jung's attitude to the spirit offered the German Jews took different forms – some, such as Eric Neumann and Hilde Kirsch, Tom Kirsch's mother, were able to get closer to their Judaism, which was affirmed through their contact with Jung. Through Jung, some of the German Jews were able to free themselves from a Judaism that was oppressive to them.

The paradoxical affinity of the truth that many Jews could find a spiritual "home" in Jung and not in Freud upends the conventional wisdom of the Jung/Freud split and the Jung/Jewish connection. Freud was far more anti-Semitic than Jung in a religious sense, although Jung was clearly more anti-Semitic than Freud in a cultural or tribal sense. So the meshugana complex is based on the following paradoxical affinity, which differentiates between spiritual and tribal affinity: Many Jews, disaffected in one way or another from traditional Judaism, were looking for a positive relation to spirit, which, paradoxically, Jung – the alleged anti-Semite – was able to provide in a way that the anti-religious Freud – the Jew – was not. Hence, the meshugana complex, which in its play of paradoxical affinities, embodies the intense rivalries and attractions of living in between groups – ethnic, racial, psychoanalytic, and religious.

Conclusion: the meshugana complex in archetypal perspective

Early in this chapter, I mentioned my reluctance to "archetypalize" until a context of the particular had been established. I have gone from anecdotes of my individual development to more general statements about Jung and the Jewish connection. I would now like to take a final step and place the meshugana complex in an archetypal context. Anselm Kiefer's sculpture *Breaking of the Vessels*,[8] which is shown in Figure 2.1, hopefully will seep into your consciousness. This is the image I have chosen to communicate an archetypal perspective.

Figure 2.1 Breaking of the Vessels, Anselm Kiefer (© Anselm Kiefer. Reproduced with permission of Antelier Anselm Kiefer, Paris)

(https://aras.org/vision-folly-american-soul)

When I first saw this sculpture many years ago in the St. Louis Art Museum, it literally took my breath away, in one of those rare moments of instant recognition of an indwelling reality that one has always known but that has just made itself visible in the world for the first time. This astounding sculpture gets as close to the embodiment of an archetype as anything I have ever seen. *Breaking of the Vessels* is Kiefer's interpretation of the Kabbalistic, which says:

> When the world was created, the attributes of God – his mercy, wisdom, and power – were divided among ten vessels that were not strong enough to hold them, and they shattered into pieces. The "breaking of the vessels" represents the introduction of evil and the human condition into the universe. The sculpture presents symbolically the human tragedy and the cycle, which can lead to rebirth and regeneration through Tikkun, the process of bringing the broken shards back together.[9]

I ask the reader to imagine that just a small shard or two of the sculpture's broken glass fragments on the gallery floor represent Freud, Jung, and the Jewish connection. What we have been calling "paradoxical affinities" can be thought of as the forces of attraction that would bring the shards together as a part of a larger whole and as the rivalrous forces that would drive the shards apart, with each "shard" making its separate claims to divine mercy, wisdom, and power.

This splintering and fragmentation with occasional glimpses of wholeness is the nature of individual human existence, the nature of life in and between groups, and as the Kabbalah would have us believe, the nature of the created universe itself. Rarely do we experience a primal unity in any of these realms – from the most personal, in which unity can be shattered by going off to summer camp at age eight, to the historical shattering of whole tribes of people, as in Kristallnacht or the Night of Broken Glass, when the windows of synagogues and Jewish-owned storefronts were smashed by mobs of Nazi sympathizers in 1938. Kristallnacht was the inspiration for Kiefer's *Breaking of the Vessels*. The Jung/Freud splintering or the Jung/Jewish connection is a small example of the potential for such shattering and/or paradoxical affinities. As individuals, we often experience ourselves as bits and pieces that rarely come together as a whole, and all of us belong to groups that may make claims to being the whole but that are, in fact, just bits and pieces. The Kabbalistic wisdom embodied in Kiefer's *Breaking of the Vessels* offers us a vision of how to "hold" the paradoxical affinities of Jung and the Jewish connection.

Notes

1 Thomas Singer, "The Meshugana Complex," *Jung Journal: Culture & Psyche* 6, no. 1 (2012): 72–84. doi:10.1525/jung.2012.6.1.72. Reprinted by permission of C. G. Jung Institute of San Francisco, www.sfjung.org.

2 C. G. Jung, *The Red Book: Liber Novus*, ed. Sonu Shamdasani, trans. Mark Kyburz, John Peck, and Sonu Shamdasani (New York: W. W. Norton & Co., 2009), 260.

3 James Carroll, *Constantine's Sword: The Church and the Jews – A History* (New York: Mariner Books, 2001).

4 Baruch Gould served as the director and creative organizer of Extended Education Programs for the C. G. Jung Institute of San Francisco for more than a decade.

5 For at least the past two decades, the question of Jung's anti-Semitism has been the major issue in Jungian circles when the issue of Jung and Judaism surfaces. This healthy "shadow work" may now give way to ground-breaking conferences such as this one in which consideration can be given to other aspects of the relationship between Jung and Judaism without the discussion having to deny the issue of Jung's anti-Semitism or being consumed by it. Perhaps the strongest vital link between Jung and Judaism is through the connection between Jung's interest in mystical traditions and the Jewish Kabbalistic tradition.

6 Thomas Singer and Samuel L. Kimbles, *The Cultural Complex: Contemporary Jungian Perspectives on Psyche and Society* (New York: Routledge, 2004).

7 Thomas Kirsch, *The Jungians: A Comparative and Historical Perspective* (London: Routledge, 2001).

8 Three people were invaluable in tracking down the image and permission for the Kiefer sculpture: Ella Rothgangel of the St. Louis Art Museum, Jacqueline West, and Mary Wells Barron.

9 Highlights of the Collection, Saint Louis Art Museum, www.slam.org/highlights/works/23.html.

3 Trump and the American selfie

Archetypal defenses of the group spirit

From *A Clear and Present Danger: Narcissism in the Era of President Trump*, edited by Leonard Cruz and Steven Buser, Chiron, 2016. Later revised as "Trump and the American Collective Psyche" for *The Dangerous Case of Donald Trump*, edited by Bandy Lee, St. Martin's Press, 2017.[1]

> In 2015–2016, I became increasingly alarmed by the candidacy of Donald Trump. I became a student of his campaign because I could sense that he had tapped into deeper and most dangerous shadowy levels of the American collective psyche. My attunement to cultural complexes, and particularly that form of cultural complex that activates archetypal defenses of the group spirit, put me on high alert. It was my original hope that the essay would have a short half-life of a few months, mirroring Trump's time-limited appearance and quick demise on the national political stage. Unfortunately, Trump prevailed.

Part one: March 2016, Trump's selfie

Donald Trump currently is carrying around a selfie stick with the longest reach in the world. And, for a long time, America has also been carrying around a selfie stick with the longest reach in the world. In a recent trip to a town as remote as Alice Springs, in the middle of Australia, I noted the charge in the dinner conversation that shot through the roof at the very mention of Trump's name. Everybody is watching him and wondering what he is about, and he seems happy to have his image become a global dark hole, sucking up planetary time and energy (Figure 3.1).

Figure 3.1 Trump voter as a mysterious force of the universe
(https://aras.org/vision-folly-american-soul)

For the media, having Donald Trump run for president is as compelling as a terrorist bomb bringing down an airplane every day – huge, dire excitement that incites obsessive attention. After dominating daily Google searches for all of 2016, Trump was finally out-searched for a few days in late May 2016, when Americans frantically Googled *gorilla* because zookeepers at the Cincinnati Zoo shot Harambe, a seventeen-year-old lowland gorilla, after a four-year-old boy fell into the primate's enclosure (Figure 3.2).

Figure 3.2 Donald Trump vs. the Gorilla, May 2016, Google search statistics

(https://aras.org/vision-folly-american-soul)

How absurdly synchronous that Donald Trump and a gorilla were fighting it out for the nation's attention. How hungry and needy we are for stimulation! At this point, so many words have been written and spoken about Donald Trump, so many theories put forth, that I feel as if I am contributing to the pollution of the environment by adding even one more word or one more theory to the stew. But here I go because I, too, am obsessed and can't help it. I am joining the not-so-cottage industry that is riding the Trump brand.

The fact is, we are all trying to make sense of the Donald Trump phenomenon and just about everybody has become a talking head, pasting together various theories about what Donald Trump's attraction as a presidential candidate really means. Stephen Hawking, a man who knows the universe and mathematics well, is perhaps the only wise man among us when he admits to being baffled when asked on ITV's *Good Morning Britain* to explain Donald Trump: "I can't," he said. Hawking went on to comment, "He is a demagogue who seems to appeal to the lowest common denominator."

Early in the Republican primaries, *The Huffington Post*'s theory was that Trump was a buffoon. The editors pontificated that he didn't deserve coverage on the front page of their website and dismissed his candidacy as a folly that would shortly collapse. They vowed to their readers that they would only report his electioneering in the entertainment section. But the day after announcing that Trump was "entertainment," *The Huffington Post* ran a front-page story on him and has done so almost every day since, making false to their readers the promise of not giving him any more headline attention. Trump rolled over their pledge in less than twenty-four hours in the same way that he has crushed all Republican opposition. There was simply too much free-floating anger and frustration in the national psyche about the current state of affairs in the United States to be activated and exploited by a figure like Trump, who appears to have an uncanny knack for pricking sacred cows. His early attacks on *political correctness* scored a direct hit on a hugely vulnerable spot in the national psyche.

There is widespread fear in our country that things are falling apart, from our infrastructure (Flint, Michigan) to our economic position in the world economy, to our ability to maintain a high standard of living and care for all our citizens, to our vulnerability to terror attacks and other forms of socio-economic disruption from outside and within our country. Trump's unique ability to capitalize on these fears could not be ignored by *The Huffington Post* or any other newspaper, journal, television or radio show, or other form of social media. Trump has the special ability to turn his campaign and person into a marketing spectacle, an irresistible circus fueled by his inflammatory comments on everything from the Mexicans to Muslims, women, his opponents, judges, and any other ready target of his apparently endless source of deep anger, aggression, suspicions, fears, and his seemingly unparalleled gift for bullying.

Trump's foundational cries of "Get 'em outta here!!!" and "Make America great again!" are perfectly attuned to the hatreds and longings at the group level of the psyche of many Americans. No one has been able to avert their gaze or turn their cash registers away from Trump. He has managed to capture and dominate our national discourse and imagination. He has been able to mesmerize or stun nearly everyone who crosses his path, including his fellow candidates running for the Republican nomination. Les Moonves, president of CBS, speaking at a Morgan Stanley Technology, Media & Telecom Conference in San Francisco, let the cat out of the bag:

> It may not be good for America, but it's damn good for CBS. . . . Man, who would have expected the ride we're all having right now? . . . The money's rolling in, and this is fun. I've never seen anything like this, and this going to be a very good year for us. Sorry. It's a terrible thing to say. But, bring it on, Donald. Keep going.[2]

The hard-to-believe fact is that there are now many people in the United States (not just white males who didn't graduate from high school or lost their jobs to overseas manufacturing or who are *authoritarian types*) who believe Trump is good for them and that he is uniquely qualified to lead the country in a new, positive direction. The focus of this chapter is less on the narcissism of Trump or other world leaders. Rather it is more on the question of why Trump's gaudy self-parade is appealing to so many people. Trump's appeal – his apparent money, power, and celebrity status, as well as his brash willingness to shoot from the hip – seems to resonate with the collective psyche of many Americans. The more vulgar his appearance and self-congratulatory his behavior and rhetoric, the more some people appear to be drawn to him. Trump's campaign has been a three-ring circus of peddling Trump steaks and other bombastic poses, a charade of a campaign that looks and sounds liked a staged wrestling match, and it is working. That it is working says something about the tastes, the intelligence, and the needs of many Americans. Of course, what I and others see as Trump's *narcissism* and his self-aggrandizing display of opulent wealth and brute power, others see as success and the ultimate achievement of the American Dream (Figure 3.3).

Figure 3.3 "Just Close Your Eyes and Pretend He's an Elephant," cartoon by Kevin Kallaugher (KAL), *Baltimore Sun*, June 5, 2016 (www.kaltoons.com)
(https://aras.org/vision-folly-american-soul)

The Trump/anti-Trump showdown has become a kind of cultural complex, in which the major attraction is surprisingly not so much Trump himself as a person but the national psychodrama playing itself out in the collective psyches of various groups in the country and their differing projections onto Trump, for which he is a perfect hook. *The Huffington Post* was not able to honor its high-ground stance to its readers to keep Trump off the front page any more than Trump presumably would be able to honor his promise, if elected president, to build a wall on the border between the United States and Mexico and have Mexico pay for it. But Trump's presence in the political arena has been all-consuming and has drawn to himself a kind of possession of the national and international psyche that defies reason. His manna has been a powerful medicine if you are for him or a truly toxic poison if you are against him. It is almost impossible for me to imagine what it feels like from the inside to embrace Trump. But, in a way, that is the challenge of trying to understand this irrational possession, whatever we label it and whatever origins or causes we attribute to it. There have been as many theories about Donald Trump's magnetic appeal or revulsion as there are theories about the causes of schizophrenia. Schizophrenia is not a bad analogy because Trump's candidacy has further revealed and amplified deep splits in the psyche of the country (and many parts of the world). For those of us profoundly disgusted and frightened by Trump – from his physical appearance and mannerisms to his worldview to his apparent beliefs and policies – it takes a considerable effort to understand or find empathy for those who have joined his movement. What causes a significant portion of our population to see Trump as a hope for America's and the world's future? That is the challenge of this chapter, which, Dear Reader, you must consider as a work in progress, as the verbal equivalent of a collage. The events and themes of riding the Trump rollercoaster are unfolding on a daily basis, and, for the individual, it is like being carried away by a flood in which one is lucky to come up for air just long enough to get a breath before being pushed under again.

Post-election reflection: December 2016

> For, after all, how do we know that two and two make four? Or that the force of gravity works? Or that the past is unchangeable? If both the past and the external world exist only in the mind, and if the mind itself is controllable – what then?
>
> George Orwell, *Nineteen Eighty-Four*[3]

Retrospectively, it is an indisputable fact that Donald Trump came to dominate every political stage he was on, including the three presidential debates that he "lost" to Hillary Clinton at which his inarticulate, restless stalking of Clinton, if not his debating skills or knowledge of the issues, were the center of attention. It is hard to forget from those debates Trump's expression of pseudo-gravitas, when he looked as though he was trying to appear serious and thoughtful. Throughout the interminable election, Trump evoked huge, inchoate, emotional energies that ranged from adoration to disdain and loathing. He remained the constant center of the political energy field – a skill that he has cultivated over a lifetime of selling himself and his projects to others. Trump won the national election by a margin of only 80,000 more votes than Hillary Clinton in three critical Midwestern states, despite losing the national popular vote to Clinton by close to 3,000,000 votes. But Trump won the national energy or libido sweepstakes by far. When all the words uttered for and against Trump have drifted away and are long forgotten, it was Donald Trump who tapped into subterranean levels of the national psyche and harnessed enormous reserves of energy in the form of rage, fear, and dread that far exceeded the psychic dynamism of all the other candidates combined. Like a black hole, Donald Trump took possession of the nation's emotional life.

Part two: blind monks describing an elephant

Trying to understand Trump reminds me of the well-known story from the Indian subcontinent of several blind monks touching an elephant to learn what it is like (Figure 3.4). But each touches a different part of its huge body, and the monks are in complete disagreement about what the elephant is. Trump is our elephant, and even though he says he's a Republican, he hardly acts like one.

Figure 3.4 Blind Men Appraising an Elephant, by Ohara Donshu, Edo period, early nineteenth century

(https://aras.org/vision-folly-american-soul)

Before putting forth my own theory, I want to offer a brief survey of some of the more interesting commentaries that have surfaced, variations of which have appeared just about everywhere. Each day, it seems, there is some new *take* on what Trump is really all about – both as a person and as a cultural/political phenomenon. I have divided these theories into various categories that might be helpful in terms of how to approach this beast.

The demographics of early Trump supporters

The most basic information about Trump's early appeal came from demographic studies that gave clear indicators about Trump's core constituency. One sure thing is that the early Trump supporters who created the emotional energy and momentum for his surprising emergence as the dominant Republican candidate will be diluted considerably, as that core constituency will be joined by most traditional Republicans (and other Hillary Clinton haters) who will present a much broader and more varied demographic profile in terms of income, socioeconomic position, and so on. In other words, Trump is going to have far more support than one would have imagined at the outset. Initially, the typical Trump supporter was white, lacked a high school diploma, had been born in the United States, frequently lived in a mobile home, had an *old economy job* (agriculture, construction, manufacturing trade), often had a segregationist voting record, and quite likely was an Evangelical Christian. *The New York Times* published a chart of the profile of early Trump supporters that can be found on its site.[4]

The character type of Trump supporters

Various notions of what motivates a Trump supporter have been put forward. Matthew MacWilliams, writing in *Politico*, argues that gender, age, income, race, or religion are not reliable predictors of an individual being a Trump supporter:

> Only two of the variables I looked at were statistically significant: authoritarianism, followed by fear of terrorism, though the former was far more significant than the latter. Authoritarianism is not a new, untested concept in the American electorate. Since the rise of Nazi Germany, it has been one of the most widely studied ideas in social science. While its causes are still debated, the political behavior of authoritarians is not. Authoritarians obey. They rally to and follow strong leaders. And they respond aggressively to outsiders, especially when they feel threatened. From pledging to "*make America great again*" by building a wall on the border to promising to close mosques and ban Muslims from visiting the United States, Trump is playing directly to authoritarian inclinations.[5]

About authoritarian types, Dan B. McAdams writes in *The Atlantic*:

> During and after World War II, psychologists conceived of the authoritarian personality as a pattern of attitudes and values revolving around adherence to society's traditional norms, submission to authorities who personify or reinforce those norms, and antipathy – to the point of hatred and aggression – toward those who either challenge in-group norms or lie outside their orbit. Among white Americans, high scores on measures of authoritarianism today tend to be associated with prejudice against a wide range of *out-groups*, including homosexuals, African Americans, immigrants, and Muslims. Authoritarianism is also associated with suspiciousness of the humanities and the arts, and with cognitive rigidity, militaristic sentiments, and Christian fundamentalism.[6]

Trump's character

Obviously, Trump's character has also been the object of many articles. The most thorough and thoughtful that I have seen is the one by McAdams in *The Atlantic*. His conclusions include the observations that Trump is a *highly extroverted, remarkably disagreeable, socially ambitious, very aggressive, angry, vigilant, fierce, tough, disciplined, narcissistic warrior*, with a desire *to win at any cost*. McAdams also observes that Trump seems to lack, or is not burdened by, the capacity for self-reflection and is apparently without a meaningful vision for himself or the country beyond his winning the presidency. It is well worth reading McAdams's complete analysis of Trump, as he combines both a trained psychological and historical perspective. About a possible Trump presidency, he writes the following:

> In sum, Donald Trump's basic personality traits suggest a presidency that could be highly combustible. One possible yield is an energetic, activist president who has a less than cordial relationship with the truth. He could be a daring and ruthlessly aggressive decision maker who desperately desires to create the strongest, tallest, shiniest, and most awesome result – and who never thinks twice about the collateral damage he will leave behind. Tough. Bellicose. Threatening. Explosive.[7]

McAdams, along with many others, has the impression that

> Trump is always playing a role – *Trump playing Trump* – and that the *real* Donald Trump remains elusive, mysterious, and perhaps doesn't even exist. Maybe he is a new kind of 21st-century personality, a character given over entirely to brand, illusion, and hyperbole – a reality TV character. . . . Who, really, is Donald Trump? What's behind the actor's mask? I can discern little more than narcissistic motivations and a complementary personal narrative about winning at any cost. It is as if Trump has invested so much of himself in developing and refining his socially dominant role that he has nothing left over to create a meaningful story for his life, or for the nation. *It is always Donald Trump playing Donald Trump*, fighting to win, but never knowing why.[8]

Post-election reflection: December 2016 – bullying, lying,
grandiosity, emotional manipulation

Trump's larger-than-life character, his grandiosity, his bullying, his indifference to facts, his insatiable need to focus all attention on himself and his own triumphs, and his seemingly unlimited capacity to tap into and exploit the vulnerabilities of our wounded national psyche pose an enormous danger to the well-being of our American republic. All these character traits were amply evident in the primaries. There was hope that in the general election Trump might show the flexibility of character to "pivot" toward the center once he had secured the right and so-called alt-right. But as the election ground on, it seemed more and more apparent that Trump's character is quite rigidly fixed in its impulsivity and narcissistic demands – and that he would stay "true" to his angry base. Trump himself seems to be governed almost exclusively by the need to win and to denigrate those who get in his way. He made it perfectly clear that he doesn't intend to change himself for anyone, and even more importantly, it is highly unlikely that he could change himself even if he wanted to. Donald Trump is all about Donald Trump. He has now successfully identified himself with a significant portion of the American population that has reciprocally identified itself with him, and anybody who doesn't accept Trump's definition of America is either "corrupt" (such as the "corrupt media") or a "loser." His inaugural baseball hat might well read "What's good for Donald Trump is good for America" as a sequel to "Make America great again." A heretofore unimaginable reality has emerged: The president-elect of the United States has tweeted himself into the position of being the most powerful cyberbully in the world. He has mastered the tweet as a high-tech bully pulpit and shown himself capable of using it in an absolutely reckless and indiscriminate way. Each of us has to ask, in fear and trembling: "Where is all of this going to lead?" The question itself suggests a perilousness to our national and international situation that is well represented by Chester Arnold's painting *Departure* (Figure 3.5).

Figure 3.5 Chester Arnold, *Departure*, 2016

(https://aras.org/vision-folly-american-soul)

The state of our culture

Three commentators have caught my attention by placing Trump's candidacy in a cultural context. Andrew Sullivan, writing in *New York* magazine, lays out a disturbingly insightful theory that Trump represents the kind of leadership that emerges in the end stages of democracy. In "Democracies End When They Are Too Democratic," Sullivan hearkens back to his early readings of Plato, in which Socrates says that "tyranny is probably established out of no other regime than democracy." Sullivan goes on to elaborate:

> What did Plato mean by that? Democracy, for him . . . was a political system of maximal freedom and equality, where every lifestyle is allowed and public offices are filled by a lottery. And the longer a democracy lasted . . . the more democratic it would become. . . . Deference to any sort of authority would wither; tolerance of any kind of inequality would come under intense threat; and multiculturalism and sexual freedom would create a city or a country like "a many-colored cloak decorated in all hues."

This rainbow-flag polity, Plato argues, is, for many people, the fairest of regimes. The freedom . . . has to be experienced to be believed – with shame and privilege in particular emerging over time as anathema. But it is inherently unstable. As the authority of elites fades, as Establishment values cede to popular ones, views and identities can become so magnificently diverse as to be mutually uncomprehending. And when all the barriers to equality . . . have been removed; when everyone is equal; when elites are despised and full license is established to do *whatever one wants*, you arrive at what might be called late-stage democracy. . . . And it is when a democracy has ripened . . . that a would-be tyrant will often seize his moment. He is usually of the elite but has a nature in tune with the time – given over to random pleasures and whims, feasting on plenty of food and sex, and reveling in the nonjudgment that is democracy's civil religion. He makes his move by "*taking over a particularly obedient mob.*" . . . If not stopped quickly, his appetite for attacking the rich on behalf of the people swells further . . . his elite enemies, shorn of popular legitimacy, find a way to appease him or are forced to flee. . . . It's as if he were offering the addled, distracted, and self-indulgent citizens a kind of relief from democracy's endless choices and insecurities. He rides a backlash to excess – *too much freedom seems to change into nothing but too much slavery* – and offers himself as the personified answer to the internal conflicts of the democratic mess. He pledges, above all, to take on the increasingly despised elites. And as the people thrill to him as a kind of solution, a democracy willingly, even impetuously, repeals itself.[9]

The second author whose trenchant analysis of American culture has caught my interest is Christopher Hedges, in his prophetic 2009 book *Empire of Illusion: The End of Literacy and the Rise of Spectacle*. I find myself in sad agreement with his observations about who we have become as a people and a nation. First, Hedges dissects how we increasingly have lost the capacity to distinguish illusion from reality in our private and public lives:

We are a culture that has been denied, or has passively given up, the linguistic and intellectual tools to cope with complexity, to separate illusion from reality. We have traded the printed word for the gleaming image. Public rhetoric is designed to be comprehensible to a ten-year-old child with a sixth grade reading level. Most of us speak at this level, are entertained and think at this level. We have transformed our culture into a vast replica of Pinocchio's Pleasure Island, where boys were lured with the promise of no school and endless fun. They were all however, turned into donkeys – a symbol, in Italian culture, of ignorance and stupidity. . . . When a nation becomes unmoored from reality, it retreats into a world of magic. Facts are accepted or discarded according to the dictates of preordained cosmology. The search for truth becomes irrelevant. Our national discourse is dominated by manufactured events, from celebrity gossip to staged showcasing of politicians to elaborate entertainment and athletic spectacles. All are sold to us through the detailed personal narratives of those we watch.

Pseudo-events – dramatic productions orchestrated by publicists, political machines, television, Hollywood, or advertisers . . . have the capacity to appear real, even though we know they are staged. They are effective because they can evoke a powerful emotional response which overshadows reality and replaces it with a fictional narrative that often becomes accepted as truth.[10]

If our unwillingness and inability to sort our illusion from reality is not enough in itself, it gets further hopelessly entangled with our cult of celebrity. Hedges does not spare us the dire consequences of our intoxication and possession with celebrity:

Celebrity culture plunges us into a moral void. No one has any worth beyond his or her appearance, usefulness, or ability to *succeed*. The highest achievements in a celebrity culture are wealth, sexual conquest, and fame. It does not matter how these are obtained. These values, as Sigmund Freud understood, are illusory. They are hollow. They leave us chasing vapors. They urge us toward a life of narcissistic self-absorption. They tell us that existence is to be centered on the practices and desires of the self rather than the common good. The ability to lie and manipulate others is held up as the highest good. The cult of self dominates our cultural landscape. This cult has within it the classic traits of the psychopaths: superficial charm, grandiosity, and self-importance; a need for constant stimulation, a penchant for lying, deception and manipulation, and the inability to feel remorse or guilt. It is the misguided belief that personal style and personal advancements, mistaken for individualism, are the same as democratic equality. We have a right, in the cult of the self, to get whatever we desire. We can do anything, even belittle and destroy those around us, including our friends, to make money, to be happy, and to become famous. Once fame and wealth are archived, they become their own justification, their own morality. How one gets there is irrelevant. Once you get there, those questions are no longer asked.[11]

If you didn't know otherwise, you would assume that Hedges is sketching a portrait of Trump, the Republican candidate, in the preceding description. But Hedges's analysis of our cult of celebrity was written in 2009, well before Trump's full-blown emergence on the national scene as a presidential candidate. Rather, Hedges is describing a generic kind of celebrity – whether politician, businessman, actor, or athlete. And generic celebrity is at the heart of our social, political, and cultural life. He is describing all of us, who we are as a people, who many of us would like to be.

Finally, the third author, Robert Reynolds, a former congressional staff person, former trustee of the Marin Community Foundation, and former Republican, offers this cogent analysis:

> Trump has survived the rhetorical equivalent of spitting on the Constitution and the American flag and yet he marches on with thousands flocking to his events and turning out to vote for him? So who are these people who are so angry that they would seemingly be willing to tear down the foundations of our government and social order and elect a man so manifestly unqualified to be President? Here in California and the salons of Manhattan and Washington it is said dismissively that the Trump supporters live in the *flyover places*. They are out of work and angry. They just don't understand or care about the consequences if Trump is actually elected. And that is exactly the point. This was the case in the late sixties when angry, disenfranchised blacks burned down their own neighborhoods and major cities in a stampede of violence and rage. They believed that it did not matter; they had lost hope and so they chanted, "*Burn, Baby! Burn!*" This is the case with much of the Arab world that feels betrayed and threatened by modernity. These red-blooded American Jihadists are willing to blow the country up in a nihilistic rage because they feel out of place and betrayed by a 21st century that has only brought war and diminished expectations.
>
> We are seeing two sides of the same coin in Trump and Sanders. It is the yin and yang of disenchantment with the establishment and its inability to address the needs of the common man. People, especially whites from the 20th century, have come to recognize that they are underserved by the old order and they are being left with less materially than they had expected. The promises and policies of both the Democrats and Republicans have been unfulfilled. Nothing incurs wrath and hatred like the imposition of lowered expectations. The rich get richer

and everyone else gets angry. The anger is particularly pronounced among Republicans who have been distracted for over a decade by the social issues of gay marriage and abortion while their economic well-being was eroding from the march of technology and global competition. Then with the Great Recession of 2008, fortunes were lost in the form of collapsed housing values, vanished 401ks and a new President who ran on the platform of Hope and delivered a sclerotic recovery and a continuing decade of war. The social issues that held them in electoral bondage proved to be a chimera; their marriages did not collapse as a consequence of gay marriage. Their marriages are collapsing because both husband and wife have to work two jobs to help support their kids who are saddled with college debt and are still unemployed. The massive income disparity infecting the country is mirrored by a mounting disparity in expectations. This will not end well. Meanwhile, many of the dividend-receiving upper middle class are living in comfort but watching the rise of Trump with horror. Some, who begin to understand how they are complicit in creating this debacle, are beginning to engage in a full-fledged naked belly crawl stampede out of the dark fetid cave that became the Republican Party.[12]

Part three: a psychological theory about Trump's appeal. A marriage of shadow, archetypal defenses, and self at the group level of the psyche to form a cultural complex

I am now going to add my own theory to all the others – each of which, like the blind monks describing the elephant, have partial claim to some truth. And I hope that on November 9, 2016, the day after the United States presidential election, that all of these theories and words – including my own – will become an irrelevant footnote to an absurd chapter in American history. I hope that the illusion of Trump that is becoming all too real will vaporize back into insubstantiality. But even if Trump vanishes from sight (an unlikely possibility), what his candidacy has revealed will not. Those who have hoped for some sort of redemption through him will still be disenfranchised and angry.

You don't need to be a psychologist or psychiatrist to see Donald Trump as a narcissist. Ted Cruz – apparently not the most psychologically minded politician – relieved any mental health professional wary of a lawsuit for character assassination of that burden by announcing on May 3, 2016, the day of the Indiana Republican Presidential primary, that Trump was "*a pathological liar, utterly amoral, a narcissist at a level I don't think this country's ever seen* and *a serial philanderer.*"[13]

But it is not Trump's narcissism that captures my attention as much as the narcissistic injury at the level of the group Self that I hypothesize about those who are so captivated by him. My focus then is not so much on Trump himself but on how his personality seems to strike such a resonant chord in many Americans and speaks to what we can think of as the group psyche. In a series of papers over the past decade, I have explored various aspects of the group psyche and have developed a working model that may be useful in understanding Trump's appeal at this time. Keep in mind that, in the following remarks, I am talking about the psyche of the *group* – what lives inside each of us as individual carriers of the group psyche and what lives between us in our shared group psyche. This group psyche engages with themes and conflicts that are not the same as our more personal psychological struggles. For better or worse, we all swim in a shared bath of collective psyche.

I want to explore what I perceive as a direct link between Trump's personal narcissism, grandiosity, and his attacks on various minority groups and the frightening growth in the number of American citizens who embrace Trump's perception of America and who feel that he understands and speaks to them. The following discussion is not a political analysis. It is a psychological analysis of the *group psyche*, which of course fuels and contributes enormously to political processes. But it is fundamentally about psyche and is based on the notion that there are certain psychological energies, even structures, at the level of the cultural or group psyche that are partly conscious and partly unconscious which are activated at times of heightened threats or perceived threats to the core identity of the group – what we might think of as the group Self. Three of these most important energies/structures are the shadow, archetypal defenses of the group Self, and the group Self itself.[14] I do not see these energies/structures as fixed entities but more as potential, dynamically shifting channels in the collective psyche through which huge affects and energies may pour when aroused. These energies/structures take shape around social, political, economic, geographic, and religious themes that are alive in specific contexts and with particular contents. This same type of analysis may currently apply in the Brexit crisis in Great Britain or in the Palestinian–Israeli conflict, with very different contexts and contents in which various groups can be seen as protecting their imagined or real, threatened, or wounded Self from being further injured by pursuing a defensive, aggressive attack against the dangerous enemy, which might be the European Union or the Palestinians – or, vice versa, the Israelis.

What is it about Trump that acts as an irresistible magnet, sucking up most of the air in our cultural psyche, both drawing people to him or repelling them from him with such ferocious attraction or repulsion? Is Trump the end product of our culture of narcissism? Is he what we get and per-haps even deserve because he epitomizes the god or gods that we currently worship in our mindless, materialistic, consumerist, hyper-indulged cult of around-the-clock stimulation and entertainment? Here is how Christopher Hedges states it:

> An image-based culture communicates through narratives, pictures, and pseudo-drama. Scandalous affairs, hurricanes, untimely deaths, train wrecks – these events play well on computer screens and televi-sion. International diplomacy, labor union negotiations, and convoluted bailout packages do not yield exciting personal narratives or stimulat-ing images. A governor who patronizes call girls becomes a huge news story. A politician who proposes serious regulatory reform advocating curbing wasteful spending is boring. Kings, queens, and emperors once used their court to divert their subjects. Today, cinematic, political, and journalistic celebrities distract us with their personal foibles and scandals. They create our public mythology. Acting, politics, and sports have become, as they were in Nero's reign, interchangeable. In an age of images and entertainment, in an age of instant emotional gratifica-tion, we neither seek nor want honesty or reality. Reality is compli-cated. Reality is boring.
>
> We are incapable or unwilling to handle its confusion. We ask to be indulged and comforted by clichés, stereotypes, and inspirational messages that tell us we can be whoever we seek to be, that we live in the greatest country on earth, that we are endowed with superior moral and physical qualities, and that our future will always be glorious and prosperous, either because of our own attributes or our national charac-ter or because we are blessed by God. In this world, all that matters is the consistency of our belief systems. The ability to amplify lies ["fake news," "deep state"], to repeat them and have surrogates repeat them in endless loops of news cycles, gives lies and mythical narratives the aura of uncontested truth. We become trapped in the linguistic prison of incessant repetition. We are fed words and phrases like *war on terror* or *pro-life* or *change* and within these narrow parameters, all complex thought, ambiguity, and self-criticism vanish.[15]

It seems clear that Trump's apparent narcissism and his attacks on political correctness dovetail with deep needs in a significant portion of the Ameri-can population to enhance their own dwindling sense of their place in the world and of America's place in the world. Trump's peculiar brand of nar-cissism is a perfect compensatory mirror for the narcissistic needs and inju-ries of those who support him. Or, stated another way, there is a good fit between Trump's personal narcissism and the narcissism of our culture and the wounded collective Self of many Americans.

With this general formulation in mind, I want to analyze how Trump's candidacy speaks to three highly intertwined parts of the American group psyche:

- To a woundedness at the core of the American group Self
- To the defenses mobilized in the groups that feel wounded who wish to protect themselves and the country against further injury to the shared group Self
- To the promise or hope of a cure for the wound

Wound to the American group self

I would first like to address what I perceive as a wound at the core of the American group Self/spirit that is deeply felt by many, especially by those who have neither benefited from nor participated in the relative well-being of our nation's prosperity and by others who are relatively well off but keenly aware that our system of government and our way of life are threatened at the core of our collective being. Here is a working definition of the group Self or spirit that I put forth in an earlier paper:

> The group spirit is akin to what we Jungians might call the *Self* of the group. The *group spirit* is the ineffable core beliefs or sense of identity that bind people together. Sports teams have a *group spirit* and their fans often magically participate in it. Nation states have a *group spirit* and their citizens often magically and unconsciously participate in it – particularly in times of crisis. Religious faiths have a *group spirit*, often symbolized by a part human/part divine being. Ethnic groups, gender groups, and racial groups all have a *group spirit* that is frequently felt and identified with in a myriad of ways. The group spirit can be symbolized by animals, humans, inanimate objects and, in its most ineffable form, the refusal to symbolize it in imagery at all. The group spirit has many different elements that have come together in a seamless, often wordless and even imageless, non-material whole that is known to its members through a sense of belonging, shared essential beliefs, core historical experiences of loss and revelation, deepest yearnings, and ideals. One can begin to circle around the nature of a group's spirit by asking questions such as:

> What is most sacred to the group?
> What does the group treasure most?
> What binds the group's members together?[16]

The group *Self* is best expressed through a symbolic image, which, in today's United States, often looks more like a brand that its creators hope will become a symbol, as represented by Trump's distinctive red "Make America Great Again," or MAGA, hat (Figure 3.6).

Figure 3.6 Trump hat: Make America Great Again

(https://aras.org/vision-folly-america-west)

Because a group's Self has so many pieces, many of which are contradictory, only an authentic symbol has a numinous quality that can contain all the tensions and conflicts. An authentic symbolic image can make a whole of the disparate parts, as does the American flag (Figure 3.7).

Figure 3.7 Jasper Johns' *Flag*, 3′ 6″ × 5′ 1″, 1954–1955

(https://aras.org/vision-folly-america-west)

Many in our country – on the left, right, and in the center – feel the country is in danger and may be beyond hope of being repaired or getting back on *the right course*. Profoundly divided, our group spirit at this stage in our history is less secure than it has been for some time. This nervousness about our essential well-being is deeply felt both by the progressive left and by the conservative right – those who feel alienated and angered by the current governing leaders (congressional, executive, and judicial branches of government) whom they oppose and see as destroying the country, whether the archenemy be Mitch McConnell of the Republicans or Barack Obama of the Democrats. On the right, the threat of terrorism (Muslims), the threat of immigrants (Mexicans), the threat of the global economy (China and international trade agreements), or the threat of our existing governing bodies and leaders (Congress) are seen as leading us to the brink. On the left, the threats to a sense of well-being and security in our national group Self come as the result of the growing disparity in the distribution of wealth and income; the mistreatment of minorities, whether those of different races, colors, ethnicities, sexual identities, or genders; our power relationships to other countries around the world; and, of course, the treatment of the environment itself.

I postulate that these threats are amplified on all sides by an even deeper, less conscious threat that I call *extinction anxiety*. Extinction anxiety exists both in the personal and group psyche and, at this time, is based on the fear of the loss of white America as we have idealized it, the loss of America's place in the world as we have known it, and ultimately the destruction of the environment and the world itself. One might think of extinction anxiety as the cultural psyche's equivalent of the anxiety about death in the individual.

I believe that this extinction anxiety is like a psychic radioactive background in our global society and that it fuels many of our concerns – whether we favor Clinton or Trump or neither. For instance, climate change deniers on the right may be seen as denying the very real possibility of the planet's destruction as a way of defending themselves against the fear of extinction. Aligning himself with this attitude, Trump offers to dispel *extinction anxiety* by denying it is real and appointing a well-known climate change denier as his energy adviser. As we all know, denial – whether at the individual or group level – is the most primitive defense in the psyche's arsenal of defenses to protect itself. This is not just about death of the individual – Freud's death instinct – this is about death of all life as we know it. This extinction anxiety belongs to all of us – to the collective psyche.

Here is how Joseph Epstein described the injury to the group Self/spirit of those attracted to Trump:

Something deeper, I believe, is rumbling behind the astounding support for Mr. Trump, a man who, apart from his large but less than pure business success, appears otherwise entirely without qualification for the presidency. I had a hint of what might be behind the support for him a few weeks ago when, on one of the major network news shows, I watched a reporter ask a woman at a Trump rally why she was supporting him. A thoroughly respectable-seeming middle-class woman, she replied without hesitation: *I want my country back.*

This woman is easily imagined clicking through TV news channels or websites and encountering this montage: Black Lives Matters protesters bullying the latest object of their ire; a lesbian couple kissing at their wedding ceremony; a mother in Chicago weeping over the death of her young daughter, struck by an errant bullet from a gang shootout; a panel earnestly discussing the need for men who *identify* as women to have access to the public lavatories of their choosing; college students, showing the results of their enfeebling education, railing about imagined psychic injuries caused by their professors or fellow students.

I don't believe that this woman is a racist, or that she yearns for immigrants, gays and other minorities to be suppressed, or even that she truly expects to turn back the clock on social change in the U.S. What she wants is precisely what she says: her country back. The political rise of Donald Trump owes less to the economy, to his status as a braggadocio billionaire, to his powers of insult, to the belief that he can Make America Great Again, than to the success of this progressive program. What the woman who said she wants her country back really meant was that she couldn't any longer bear to watch the United States on the descent, hostage to progressivist ideas that bring neither contentment nor satisfaction but instead foster a state of perpetual protest and agitation, anger and tumult. So great is the frustration of Americans who do not believe in these progressivist ideas, who see them as ultimately tearing the country apart, that they are ready to turn, in their near hopelessness, to a man of Donald Trump's patently low quality.[17]

The Self or group spirit of America is built on more than three hundred years of progress, success, achievement, resourcefulness, and ingenuity, accompanied by almost endless opportunity and good fortune. We love and believe in our heroic potential; our freedom and independence; our worship of height and speed, youth, newness; technology; our optimism; and our eternal innocence. We have enjoyed the profound resilience of the American spirit, which has shown itself repeatedly through difficult historical trials, including our Civil War, World War I, the Great Depression, World War II, the Vietnam War, the 9/11 attacks, the Iraq War, the financial collapse in 2008, and other major crises. As a country, we have been blessed in our capacity to transcend loss, failure, and the threat of defeat in the face of crisis time and again, and this has contributed to a positive vision of ourselves that for a long time has been fundamentally solid at the core. Of course, that Self-image is subject to inflation, arrogance, and grandiosity in our belief in our own exceptionalism and our blindness to our causing grave injury to other peoples at home and abroad. Again, this Self-image exists at the level of the group psyche. It is quite possible that Trump's personal inflation, arrogance, and grandiosity represents a compensatory antidote in our group psyche to a Self-image beginning to suffer severe self-doubt about our ability to navigate a highly uncertain future successfully and the nostalgic longing perfectly articulated in the phrase: "*I want my country back.*"

Archetypal defenses of the group self

Second are the defenses mobilized by those feeling this woundedness who wish to protect themselves and their country against further injury to the shared group spirit. A significant number of people in our society feel cut off from what they believe to be their inherited, natural birthright as American citizens. Those for whom our cherished American group spirit seems endangered are ready to defend themselves – whether the perceived attack is coming from within or outside the country. Although they would not use this language, they are suffering a wound at the level of the group spirit or Self, even as they are also suffering individually. We can think of this as a narcissistic injury at the level of our group Self. I suggest that Trump has somehow intuited that injury and is playing to it, both as a carrier of the renewal of the group spirit and as a defender against those who would do further harm to it – be it terrorists; immigrants; Washingtonian political insiders; the established Republican Party; Obama; and, perhaps above all else right now, Hillary Clinton and the Democrats.

Trump's attack on political correctness

Trump's particular political genius in this election cycle has been to launch his campaign with an attack on *political correctness*. With incredible manipulative skill, Trump's full-throated yawp of a barbarian New Yorker, *"Get 'em outta here!"*, made its first appearance at his rallies when he urged the faithful in his crowds to get rid of protesters (one can't help but wonder if these *protesters* weren't, in fact, paid actors planted in the crowd). *"Get 'em outta here!"* also seems to be his pledge to rid the country of Mexicans, Muslims, and other groups that were portrayed as dangerous threats to the American Way of Life. His sneering attacks on *political correctness* and his willingness time and again to be *politically incorrect* have tapped into the shadowy feelings that many have about all the things they are supposed to be compassionate about – ethnic differences, racial differences, color differences, gender differences, religious differences. Trump's strategy has been shrewd. He seems to have sensed that *political correctness* could be the trigger word and target for unleashing potent levels of shadow energies that have been accumulating in the cultural unconscious of the group psyche. He rode a huge wave of pent-up resentment, racism, and hatred unleashed by his attacks on *political correctness* long enough to crush his Republican opponents and become the Republican nominee for president of the United States. The notion of a trigger word activating a complex goes back to Jung's early word association tests in which certain words detonated powerful emotions contained within personal complexes – such as the mother or father complex. Cultural complexes are also frequently triggered by a collective word association process that takes on a life of its own in the psyche of the group and that can be manipulated by skillful politicians who use specific trigger words to activate the primitive emotions that fuel cultural complexes. Trump is at his best when he is awful.

Trump's willingness to be politically incorrect has become a sign of his "truth-telling" to many. Trump embodies the truth of the shadow side of political correctness and that seems to be the primary truth that his core followers care about. Once Trump spoke to their emotional truth, the Trump faithful no longer cared whether he told other truths. Cultural complexes don't need or rely on facts to validate their particular perspective on the world. If it feels right, it must be so. In fact, it is a characteristic of cultural complexes that facts are just about the first thing to go when an individual or group becomes possessed by a complex. A group caught up in a cultural complex has highly selective memory – if any historical memory at all – and only chooses those historical and contemporary *facts* that validate their pre-existing opinion. In a wild inversion from Trump's seemingly frequent misrepresentation of the truth, people have apparently come to believe that Trump is *"telling it like it is"* in his attacks on the inept Washington politicians who know nothing about conducting business. For instance, in full tricksterish play with the truth, Trump glibly dismissed taped recordings of his own voice before the 2008 housing market collapse, pronouncing that he looked forward to a fall in prices as it represented a great buying opportunity for him at low prices. He said any good businessman would have looked for such an opportunity, and the movie *The Big Short* (2015) gives ample evidence of those who profited from others' traumatic losses.[18] As infuriating as it is that facts don't seem to make any difference in Trump's self-presentation, it would be a huge mistake to underestimate how successfully he has mobilized the crude underbelly of long-standing American suspicions of people who are different from themselves. What a relief for so many to hear a politician speak their unspoken resentments and express their rage, which they could only mutter privately. Trump apparently tapped into the dirty little (or not so little) secret of our loathing of various minorities (even though we may all be minorities now) and especially of recent immigrants.

This kind of shadow energy is much more likely to be close to the surface of consciousness and available for exploitation if a group of people who previously saw themselves as having a solid place in American society now find themselves marginalized and drifting downward – both socially and economically – or as never having had a chance of making progress toward the American Dream. In fact, they see the recent immigrants to this country as stealing the American Dream from them.

Post-election reflection, December 2016

> In a way, the world-view of the Party imposed itself most successfully on people incapable of understanding it. They could be made to accept the most flagrant violations of reality, because they never fully grasped the enormity of what was demanded of them, and were not sufficiently interested in public events to notice what was happening. By lack of understanding they remained sane. They simply swallowed everything, and what they swallowed did them no harm, because it left no residue behind, just as a grain of corn will pass undigested through the body of a bird.
>
> George Orwell, *Nineteen Eighty-Four*[19]

Donald Trump uncovered a huge sinkhole of dark raw emotions in the national psyche for all of us to see. Rage, hatred, envy, and fear surfaced in a forgotten, despairing white underclass who had little reason to believe that the future would hold the promise of a brighter life purpose. Trump's formula for repairing these deep wounds had him crusading around the country, chanting the hopeful mantra of making better "deals." And, as part of the brave new world that Trump is promising, we have been introduced to the notion that we are living in a postfactual era, which many who support Trump either cynically or glibly proclaim. Here is how I understand this "willing suspension of disbelief" when it comes to our contemporary political drama. What matters most in political battle are the competing narratives between conflicting groups of people that are often generated by cultural complexes. Once the complex takes over the narrative or the narrative gives voice to the complex's core, facts simply become irrelevant. The consequence of abandoning facts as a foundation for informed decision-making allows individuals and groups to accept "truths as lies" and "lies as truths." Inevitably, this leads to the kind of terrifying *Nineteen Eighty-Four* scenario in which

> the Ministry of Peace concerns itself with war, the Ministry of Truth with lies, the Ministry of Love with torture, and the Ministry of Plenty with starvation. These contradictions are not accidental, nor do they result from ordinary hypocrisy: they are deliberate exercises in *doublethink*. For it is only by reconciling contradictions that power can be retained indefinitely. In no other way could the ancient cycle be broken. If human equality is to be forever averted – if the High, as we have called them, are to keep their places permanently – then the prevailing mental condition must be controlled insanity.[20]

Trump's cabinet appointments suggest that this is what will soon be happening in our own government departments. The job of each new cabinet leader will be to reverse or dismantle the very reason for which his or her department exists.

Unholy marriage of shadow, archetypal defenses of the group self, and the group self

What makes Trump's unleashing of the shadow in the American psyche around political correctness even more dangerous is that these energies become linked or even identical with what I call *archetypal defenses of the group spirit*. Here is how I have defined "archetypal defenses of the group spirit":

> This phrase is a mouthful, but its purpose is to offer a precise psychological description of a level of collective emotional life that is deeply responsive to threat – whether the threat is real or simply *perceived* as real. When this part of the collective psyche is activated, the most primitive psychological forces come alive for the purpose of defending the group and its collective spirit or Self. I capitalize *Self* because I want to make it clear that it is not just the persona or ego identity of the group that is under attack but something at an even deeper level of the collective psyche which one might think of as the spiritual home or *god* of the group. The tendency to fall into the grips of an identification with an archetypal defense of the group spirit is universal, and almost every one of us has experienced such a *possession* at some time in our lives – at least in one if not many of the primary groups to which we belong simultaneously. The tribal spirit of the clan or of the nation often lies dormant or in the background, but when it is threatened, the defenses mobilized to protect it are ferocious and impersonal. The mobilization of such potent, archaic defenses is fueled by raw collective emotion and rather simplistic, formulaic ideas and/or beliefs. One can think of the more virulent cultural complexes as being fed by a vast underground pool of the collective emotional life. Archetypal defenses of the group spirit are animated by the release of these heightened emotions of groups in distress. . . . Once a certain level of emotional intensity is achieved in the psyche of the group, archetypal defenses of the group spirit come to the forefront and begin to determine and even dictate how the group will think, feel, react, and behave.

These activated archetypal defenses of the group spirit find concrete expression in forms as varied as the unrest of divided populations over the legal status of foreign immigrants in countries around the world, the threatened development of nuclear weapons by nation states such as Iran or North Korea, the deployment of suicide bombers by terrorist groups, or the launching of massive military expeditions by world powers. And, these same kinds of archetypal defenses come alive in all sorts of skirmishes between diverse groups of people, who are not necessarily armed with explosive devices but perceive themselves in a threatened or disadvantaged position in which their most sacred values are in jeopardy – Gays, Blacks, Women, the Christian Right in the United States, Jews around the world, the Muslim Brotherhood throughout the Middle East. The list of groups threatened at the core of their being or at the level of the group Self seems endless.[21]

From the point of view of the group psyche, Trump has aligned his attack on political correctness with the archetypal defenses of the group spirit. That is why I stress his two foundational mantras: "Get 'em outta here!" and "Make America great again!" – in other words, "Rid the country of all elements that threaten our sense of Self," and "Make the country white and powerful and rich again." The first statement speaks for the shadow/ archetypal defense of the group spirit, and the second statement speaks for the repair to the group Self. This constellation of group energies/structure puts the shadow very close to the Self, very close to what the group values most about itself and how it protects itself. This gives further license in the unconscious of the group to ride and act out these aggressive, hateful, and violent forces in the collective psyche. What makes Trump's narcissism so dangerous in its mix of shadow (his attacks on all sorts of groups of people) and Self elements (his self-aggrandizing, inflated sense of himself) is that it plays to the unholy marriage of Self and shadow elements in the collective psyche.

Trump's example gives permission for shadowy thoughts, feelings, and actions on behalf of the Self. I think this underlying group dynamic explains the comparison of Trump to Hitler. Evoking an archaic image of the German Self, Hitler mobilized the most shadowy forces in modern history in the so-called service of that Self-image, which centered on the supremacy of the Aryan race – first the Brownshirts, then the Gestapo, SS, and other forces of the Third Reich, including its highly efficient bureaucracy. Trump seems to be toying with the collective shadow, apparently encouraging its acting out in the name of the Self. It is hard to imagine Trump leading the United States in the same direction that Hitler led Germany (I certainly hope I don't live to regret writing these words), but the thought of the United States under the leadership of a grandiose and puffed-up character such as Trump is terrifying. From the point of view of analytical psychology, when the shadow, the archetypal defenses of the group spirit, and the group Self in any group get so closely aligned, there is great danger of violence, tyranny, and absolutism.

Most of the anger we have witnessed has been coming from Trump's supporters who join in his attacks on political correctness and immigrants. Even more dangerous in Trump's apparent indiscriminate activation of shadowy attacks on political correctness is the possibility that he will unleash equally destructive counterattacks on the other side of the equation – in those people who feel Trump's assault on them endangers their core identity and being as individuals and as groups. As of this writing (early June 2016), I believe that we have seen just the very tip of the huge store of collective emotional counter-responses to Trump. During the next several months leading up to the presidential elections, we may well witness increasing anger and violence erupting on both sides, and I sense that the fear, resentment, and hostility building up *against* Trump in the United States will be even greater than what he has mobilized on his own behalf. From those who see themselves as defending the American Self or soul against Trump, there could be increasingly virulent displays of hostility toward Trump as a compensatory counter-reaction to Trump as a false Self, to Trump as a false god, to Trump as a demagogue.

Curing the wounded self of America: Trump's selfie and America's selfie

The third and final component of this intertwined triad of forces in the group psyche is Trump's implicit promise to provide a cure for the wound at the level of the group Self. This is where Trump's narcissism is most prominent and most dangerous. I believe there is an unconscious equation between Trump's inflated sense of himself and the cure for the American group Self that many believe he promises. This equation can be most simply stated as the following: "I am the Greatness to which America may once again aspire. By identifying with how great I am, you can rekindle your wounded American dream and make yourself and America great again." Or even more bluntly, "I have achieved the American dream; I am the American dream; I am the incarnation of the Self that the country aspires to." This, of course, is a massive inflation. Trump identifies his personal being with the Self of America, and it is his source of demagogic appeal to authoritarians and others. He is encouraging those Americans who have lost a foothold in the American Dream to place their trust in him as a mirror of their own potential – a potential that he personally has already achieved. If one can place themselves in that mindset, one can get a glimpse of Trump's magnetic appeal.

Synchronistically, the day after I wrote the preceding words in an attempt to imaginatively enter into the psyche of someone drawn into Trump's orbit, I came across the following quote from Trump, a statement that he made many years ago but that applies even more today, when the stakes are much greater:

> I play to people's fantasies. People may not always think big themselves, but they can still get very excited by those who do. That's why a little hyperbole never hurts. People want to believe that something is the biggest and the greatest and the most spectacular. I call it truthful

hyperbole. It's an innocent form of exaggeration – and a very effective form of promotion.[22]

Trump's apparent money, power, fame, and his willingness to shoot from the hip seem to fit with the frustrated yearnings of many Americans. He has managed to catch the projection of a powerful and successful person who, by virtue of his alleged business acumen and ability to negotiate, is able to make things happen for his own betterment – rarely for the betterment of others, despite his claims of giving generously to charities and creating untold jobs. F. Scott Fitzgerald might roll over in his grave at this comparison, but Trump brings to mind a latter-day Jay Gatsby, whose overweening ambitions for fame, fortune, and social status are unlimited. Trump manages to project an image that he is everything Willy Loman in Arthur Miller's *Death of a Salesman* was not able to achieve. Trump has accomplished – at least in the minds of many Americans – what Jay Gatsby and Willy Loman could only dream of. In this sense, Trump presents himself as the embodiment of a form of the American Dream that, in his singular greatness and achievement, he can personally restore to America's wounded Self-image and to those Americans who have failed to achieve their dreams of greatness. It is almost as if Trump is saying, "My grandiosity is the greatness of America. We can make America great again by following me and then, you, too, can be like me: aggressive, successful, big, powerful." This has tremendous appeal for many. This is the narcissism of Trump joining with the injured narcissism of Americans who have seen their chances for well-being and security rapidly slipping away. In that sense, Trump is not only speaking for the shadow; he is also speaking for the Self of America – or, at least, his version of it. His version is the materialistic power version of the American Dream – of the big man who has made himself rich and, through his wealth and strength of personality, powerful. He is free to speak his own mind and to pursue, without limits, his own self-aggrandizing goals.

The negative aspects of Trump's narcissism strike those who have been repelled rather than attracted by him as a symbolic mirror of everything negative about America's culture of narcissism. Just as some think that Trump is the embodiment of everything that has made America great in the past and will make us great again, some see Trump as the very embodiment of everything awful that we have become as a nation. Undoubtedly, this is also what many in the rest of the world see as the worst of who we have become. In this view, we can see the shadow of the American "selfie" as

- A self-promoting brand
- Arrogant bullies in our conduct of business and other relations

- Quite limited in our capacity for self-reflection
- Filled with hubris and a lack of humility
- Self-absorbed, with little sensitivity for the needs of others
- Possessed by greed and consumerism
- So entitled in our good fortune that we have come to believe this is our natural due

These seven features are core characteristics of the American cultural complex in which the shadow, archetypal defenses of the American Spirit, and the American Self get all mixed up with each other into the most noxious stew, and we find ourselves betraying that very Self or spirit on which the nation and its constitution were founded. And how dreadful to think that Trump's narcissism is a perfect mirror and archetypal embodiment of our national narcissism. And what if it is also a mirror of our own shadowy personal narcissism, to boot? Ultimately, I believe that the Trump phenomenon is less about Trump than it is about us – about who we are as a people. From this perspective, the elephant in the room turns out to be "We the People of the United States." How terrifying to think that our politics and our lives today have gotten horribly confused with reality TV, social media, computer and cellphone technology, and their infinite capacity to turn reality into illusion, Self into narcissism.

Part four: Trump as a perverted echo of Walt Whitman

"Do I contradict myself?"

Just as F. Scott Fitzgerald and Arthur Miller have come to mind as I contemplate how Trump's narcissism plays to the injured narcissism of America's group Self, Walt Whitman – the ultimate bard of the American soul – comes to mind, as some of Whitman's words have a strange, disorienting resonance with how Trump presents himself. Several pundits have played with the notion of Donald Trump being some sort of twisted mirror image of Walt Whitman. For instance, Zenpundit sardonically points to the similarity between how Trump behaves and what Whitman says about himself in the lines:

> Do I contradict myself?
> Very well then, I contradict myself.
> (I am large, I contain multitudes.)[23]

Trump is so large and powerful that he doesn't have to be predictable. He can change his mind if he wants.

"Song of Myself"

In "Song of Myself," one of Whitman's most famous poems from *Leaves of Grass*, the poet gets as close to evoking the soul/Self of America as any American has in his visionary lines:

> I celebrate myself, and sing myself,
> And what I assume you shall assume,
> For every atom belonging to me as good belongs to you.
>
> I loafe and invite my soul,
> I lean and loafe at my ease observing a spear of summer grass.
>
> My tongue, every atom of my blood, form'd from this soil, this air,
> Born here of parents born here from parents the same, and their
>   parents the same,
> I, now thirty-seven years old in perfect health begin,
> Hoping to cease not till death.[24]

It is easy to imagine Trump also saying "I celebrate myself. I sing myself." Everything Trump says and does seems to be a celebration of himself. We know, intuitively, that Trump's "song of myself" is not the same one that Whitman sings. Trump sings a self-congratulatory song; Whitman sings a Self-affirming song. One song is of and for the whole nation; the other song centers on the triumph of Trump himself and for all those individuals who would appropriate his claim to superiority for themselves.

"I am the poet of the Body and I am the poet of Soul"

In *Leaves of Grass*, Whitman proclaims himself the bard of the American soul when he writes: "I am the poet of the Body and I am the poet of the Soul."[25] Whitman likens the body and soul of America to a blade of grass whose very existence mirrors the "journey work of the stars" in its immortality. Trump claims himself to be the body and soul of America in the Trump Casinos, the Trump Towers, Trump University, and even Trump Steaks – shoddy pretenders to what is best and most soulful in America.

"I sound my barbaric yawp over the roofs of the world"

Whitman sings his mystical, transcendent vision of America as he compares himself to the spotted hawk who soars above the sacred land:

> The spotted hawk swoops by and accuses me, he complains of my gab
>   and my loitering.

I too am not a bit tamed, I too am untranslatable,
I sound my barbaric yawp over the roofs of the world.[26]

Trump echoes these sentiments as he proudly presents himself to the world as "untranslatable." He, too, shouts his own "barbaric yawp" over the roofs of the world. In Whitman's imagination, the essence of the American soul is neither civilized nor verbal. The "barbaric yawp" is the fierce "voice" of a soul that is unrestrained and exulting in its self-expression. It gives expression to a primitive enthusiasm in the form of a nonverbal cry from the essential nature of a living being. Allen Ginsberg's *Howl* and Bob Dylan's voice, once described as "a coyote caught in barbed wire," can be considered grandchildren of Whitman's "barbaric yawp" of the American soul. So, too, is Jimi Hendrix's rendition of "The Star Spangled Banner."

I think it worthwhile to read again Steven Herrmann's quote from Chapter 1 about Whitman's barbaric yawp, against the background of Trump ten years later:

> Whitman's "yawp" is a *conscious* cry from the Soul of America to make the barbarian in American political democracy conscious! The "barbaric yawp" is Whitman's call from the depths of the American Soul to awaken the possibility of hope in a brighter future for American democracy. . . . The aim of Whitman's "barbaric yawp" was to sound a new heroic message of "Happiness," Hope, and "Nativity" over the roofs of the world, to sound a primal cry which must remain essentially "unsaid" because it rests at the core of the American soul and cannot be found in "any dictionary, utterance, symbol."[27] The "barbaric yawp" is a metaphorical utterance for something "untranslatable," a primal cry from the depths of the American Soul for the emergence of man as a spiritual human being in whom the aims of liberty and equality have been fully realized and in whom the opposites of love and violence, friendship and war, have been unified at a higher political field of order than anything we have formerly seen in America. His "yawp" is an affect state, a spiritual cry of "Joy" and "Happiness" prior to the emergence of language.[28]

Trump's "barbaric yawp" ("Get 'em outta here!") may sound tinny in comparison to those who came before him, such as Whitman, Ginsberg, Dylan, Hendrix, and many others who have tapped into a primal energy that is essentially American. At great risk, however, one could too-quickly discount the fact that Trump also has his own instinct for a primal source of American "barbaric" enthusiasm.

I cannot help but wonder if Donald Trump and his inarticulate utterances, which make so many of us cringe, have not been heard by many in America as a modern version of Whitman's "barbaric yawp" from our country's "body and soul." However reluctantly, we must accept the fact that Trump may speak directly to the American soul of many in our country, just as our more progressive sensibilities can link Barack Obama's measured oratory to the American soul. Who are we to suppose we know who speaks for the American soul? Who has a legitimate claim on the American soul anyway? Is it possible that Donald Trump has found in his crude utterances a resonance with the American soul that speaks more to many Americans' identities and yearnings than most of us can imagine?

Comparing Trump to Whitman may seem sacrilegious to the memory of the great American poet. But there is a logic to such a comparison, as Trump is the shadow or dark mirror to the best things in America, sung so eloquently by Whitman. Trump's "song of myself" is truly a "song of *myself.*" Whitman sings of what is best in us, and Trump's horrific bluster displays what is worst in us. What is sacred in Whitman's "barbaric yawp" becomes profane in Trump's perverted echo of that yawp.

I leave the reader with a question, given that I believe both Whitman and Trump identify themselves with the soul or Self of America. What is the difference between Whitman's "I celebrate myself, I sing myself" and Trump's version of that same song in "Make America great again"? It is worth grappling with this question as a way of differentiating that kind of narcissism in which the ego gets inflated and identifies with the Self and its archetypal defenses versus that kind of rare but blessed, over-flowing exuberance, integrity, and love in which the ego is connected to but not identified with the Self. What is real about Trump's selfie is the unexpurgated expression of both his own and America's grandiose, narcissistic, misogynistic, racist, materialistic, shadowy abuse of power. What is authentic about Whitman's barbaric yawp as a Self-portrait of America is its life-affirming, primitive vitality, which is not to be confused with Trump's cheesy Bronx cheer as an American selfie.

Post-election reflection, December 2016: groping the American psyche – psychic contagion

There are so many frightening consequences of an emerging Trump presidency – on the climate, on minorities, on immigration, on women's rights, on Trump's conflicts of interest, and on the possibilities of international disasters with China, Russia, Syria, Iran, and even our own allies. The list of the potential dangers goes on and on. But one of the most disturbing thoughts to me about the looming Trump presidency is that he is going to take up residence not just in the White House but also in the psyches of each and every one of us for the next several years. We are going to have to live with him rattling around inside us, all of us at the mercy of his impulsive and bullying whims, shooting from the hip at whatever gets under his skin in the moment with uninformed but cleverly calculated inflammatory shots. The way a US president lives inside each of us can feel like a very personal and intimate affair. Those who identify with Trump and love the way he needles the "elites" may relish having him live inside all of us as a reliable tormentor of those they hate, fear, and envy. Trump is very good at brutally toying with his enemies, which include women, professionals, the media, the educated classes, and minorities – to mention just a few.

What most frightens me about Trump is his masterful skill at invading and groping the national psyche. Many tired of the Clintons taking up almost permanent residence in our national psyche. Trump will soon put the Clintons to shame in his capacity to dwell in and stink up our collective inner space, like the proverbial houseguests who overstay their welcome. And many of us never invited Trump into our psychic houses in the first place. That is perhaps why the image that has stayed with me the most from the national disgrace that was our 2016 election is that of the woman who came forward to tell her alleged story of being sexually harassed by Trump. Some years ago, she was given an upgrade to first class on a plane and found herself sitting next to "The Donald." In no time at all, he was literally groping her all over – breasts and below. She describes the physicality of the assault by him as like being entangled by the tentacles of an octopus from whom she was barely able to free herself and retreat to economy class. It now feels as though we have all been groped by the tentacles of Trump's octopus-like psyche that has invaded our psyches for the past year and that threatens to tighten its squeeze on our collective psyche for at least the next four years. So we must go back to economy class and begin to prepare ourselves for battle with an octopus that will soon move into the White House. To be as vulgar as Trump himself, Trump has grabbed the American psyche by the "pussy."

As we slowly collect ourselves after this devastating and unexpected tsunami of Trump winning the presidency, I can begin to sense that many are finding renewed energy and commitment to fight for a progressive agenda that has been thoroughly derailed by Trump's victory. Hopefully, in this deep resurgence of political activism to reclaim our most cherished and threatened American values, we will not allow ourselves to once again become siloed in our own tendencies to cocoon ourselves in a self-righteous, arrogant bubble of narcissistic progressive ideals.

Notes

1 Thomas Singer, "Trump and the American Selfie: Archetypal Defenses of the Group Spirit," in *A Clear and Present Danger: Narcissism in the Era of President Trump*, ed. Leonard Cruz and Steven Buser (Asheville, NC: Chiron Publications, 2016), 25–55. Reprinted by permission of Chiron Publications. The chapter was also adapted to appear in *The Dangerous Case of Donald Trump: Text from the Dangerous Case of Donald Trump: 27 Psychiatrists and Mental Health Experts Assess the President*, © 2017 by Thomas Singer. Reprinted by permission of Thomas Dunne Books, an imprint of St. Martin's Press, New York. All Rights Reserved.

2 Eliza Collins, "Les Moonves: Trump's Run Is Damn Good for CBS," *Politico*, February 29, 2016, www.politico.com/blogs/on-media/2016/02/les-moonves-trump-cbs-220001.

3 Georg Orwell, *Nineteen Eighty-Four*, A Project Gutenberg of Australia Ebook, Ebook #010021, 75. Internet Archive, https://archive.org/details/NineteenEighty Four-Novel-GeorgeOrwell.

4 Neil Irwin and Josh Katz, "The Geography of Trumpism," *The New York Times*, March 12, 2016, www.nytimes.com/2016/03/13/upshot/the-geography-of-trumpism.html.

5 Matthew MacWilliams, "The One Weird Trait That Predicts Whether You're a Trump Supporter," *Politico Magazine*, January 17, 2017, ¶¶5–6, www.politico.com/magazine/story/2016/01/donald-trump-2016-authoritarian-213533.

6 Dan P. McAdams, "The Mind of Donald Trump," *The Atlantic*, June 2016, from "I. His Disposition," www.theatlantic.com/magazine/archive/2016/06/the-mind-of-donald-trump/480771/.

7 Ibid.

8 Ibid., IV. His Self-Conception.

9 Andrew Sullivan, "Democracies End When They Are Too Democratic," *New York*, May 2016, ¶¶1–2, 4–5, http://nymag.com/daily/intelligencer/2016/04/america-tyranny-donald-trump.html.

10 Chris Hedges, *Empire of Illusion: The End of Literacy and the Triumph of Spectacle* (New York: Nation Books, 2009), 44, 50.

11 Ibid., 32–33.

12 Ryan Reynolds, personal communication, June 2016.

13 David Wright, Tal Kopan, and Julia Manchester, "Cruz Unloads with Epic Takedown of 'Pathological Liar,' 'Narcissist' Donald Trump," *CNN Politics*, May 3, 2016, www.cnn.com/2016/05/03/politics/donald-trump-rafael-cruz-indiana/.

14 Jean Kirsch, in a personal conversation, pointed out to me that characterizing certain phenomenon in the group psyche as *energies/structures* is analogous to the development of the wave/particle duality in physics, in which every quantic entity may be partly described as a particle and partly described as a wave to fully explain the different types of behaviors they exhibit. It may be similar to discussing archetypes or culture complexes in the group psyche, which can sometimes manifest as energies and sometimes as structures.

15 Hedges, *Empire of Illusion*, 49.

16 Thomas Singer, "Unconscious Forces Shaping International Conflicts: Archetypal Defenses of the Group Spirit from Revolutionary America to Confrontation in the Middle East," *The San Francisco Jung Institute Library Journal* 25, no. 4 (2006): 9–10.

17 Joseph Epstein, "Why Trumpkins Want Their Country Back," *Wall Street Journal*, June 10, 2016, www.wsj.com/articles/why-trumpkins-want- their-country-back-1465596987.

18 *The Big Short*, directed by Adam McKay, screenplay by Adam McKay and Charles Randolph (Los Angeles: Paramount Pictures, 2015).

19 Orwell, *Nineteen Eighty-Four*, 143.

20 Ibid., 199.

21 I have patterned this model of group dynamics on Donald Kalsched's ground-breaking work on trauma and the injury to the Self in the individual, especially his *The Inner World of Trauma: Archetypal Defenses of the Personal Spirit*, but my work has focused on what we might call *The Inner World of Group Trauma: Archetypal Defenses of the Group Spirit*. I argue that this is a particular variety of what I call a *cultural complex*. See Singer, "Unconscious Forces Shaping International Conflicts."

22 Marc Fisher and Will Hobson, "Trump Masqueraded as Publicist to Brag About Himself," *Washington Post*, May 13, 2016, www.washingtonpost.com/politics/donald-trump-alter-ego-barron/2016/05/12/02ac99ec-16fe-11e6-aa55-670cabef46e0_story.html?hpid=hp_rhp-top-table-main_no-name%3Ahomepage%2Fstory.

23 Walt Whitman, *The Project Gutenberg Ebook of Leaves of Grass*, Project Gutenberg, Ebook #1322, www.gutenberg.org/ebooks/1322; Charles Cameron, "Trump as Walt Whitman," *Zenpundit.com*, May 5, 2016, http://zenpundit.com/?p=50041.

24 Walt Whitman, "Song of Myself," in *Leaves of Grass*, Project Gutenberg, www.gutenberg.org/ebooks/1322, section 1. "In the poem, Whitman emphasizes an all-powerful 'I' which serves as narrator, who should not be limited to or confused with the person of the historical Walt Whitman. The persona described has transcended the conventional boundaries of self: 'I pass death with the dying, and birth with the new-washed babe . . . and am not contained between my hat and boots' (section 7)." Wikipedia, "Song of Myself," s.v. (accessed August 15, 2019), https://en.wikipedia.org/wiki/Song_of_Myself.

25 Whitman, "Song of Myself," section 21.

26 Ibid., section 52. *Barbaric* means "without civilizing influences, primitive" and a *yawp* is a "loud, harsh cry."

27 Ibid., section 50.

28 Steven Herrmann, personal communication, January 2007.

4   If Donald Trump had a selfie stick, we'd all be in the picture

From *Moyers*, August 12, 2016.[1]

Bill Moyers read the original, much longer version of my essay on Trump, which appears in the previous chapter, and suggested that I prepare a shortened version for Moyers, *his online journal. Moyers editing my essay was a highlight of my experience as a writer.*

Figure 4.1 A supporter takes a selfie with Republican presidential candidate Donald Trump as he greets the crowd after speaking at a campaign event at JetSmart Aviation Services in Rochester, New York, on April 10, 2016. (Photo by Jabin Botsford/*The Washington Post* via Getty Images)

(https://aras.org/vision-folly-american-soul)

Because a single powerful leader will draw from the rest of us powerful projections ranging from savior to devil, from healer to destroyer, I have long been interested, as a psychiatrist and Jungian psychoanalyst, in the relationship between politics, mythology, and psychology. For people like me, this is our year.

Like many others, I didn't take Donald Trump seriously at first. Then, while traveling in Australia in the spring, I saw a young man taking pictures of himself and his girlfriend using a long selfie stick that he used to place his iPhone right in a koala bear's face. At that moment I thought of Trump. He is using the longest selfie stick in the world to project his face around the globe, stirring intense emotions in others with simplistic ideas about race, ethnicity, gender, and national security – the ingredients of what in our field we call "the group psyche." Unlike many political commentators, I spend a lot of time exploring the psyche of the group – what lives inside each of us as individual carriers of that psyche and what lives between us in our shared experience of swimming, so to speak, in the same waters of powerful collective emotions.

Each of us has taken a Trump trip over the past months; a nonstop rollercoaster ride – obsessive, compelling, endlessly dramatic, and at times outrageous and terrifying. Sometimes it seems we have crossed over into a mad incomprehensibility – as with Trump's recent suggestion that "Second-Amendment Americans" just might take care of Hillary Clinton. Like everybody else, I find myself pulled into this tug-of-war, wondering what in the world is going on even as I come close to panicking at the feeling that I am being sucked under.

Wherever he is, wherever he goes, Trump invariably draws huge attention and makes himself the center of interest. For some that can be inspiring; for others, it can be traumatizing. He is larger than life – what we sometimes call "grandiose." What especially interests me is how, in stirring up collective emotions and group issues of identity, Trump finds a seamless fit with significantly large segments of the population. Obviously, he is tapping deep currents in the American psyche that fuel our political thoughts and behavior. Some see him as a colossal narcissist, sucking up all the energy around himself like a black hole and making himself a grave threat to American life – Public Menace No. 1. Others see him as a dynamic and successful businessman who gets things done and courageously speaks unpleasant truths.

He has masterfully cultivated his celebrity, playing on our national preference for illusion over reality.

The easiest thing, of course, is to fix Trump in one's mind as just one thing – a buffoon, say, a demonic demagogue, or a savior. But he and the media circus surrounding him are far more complex than any one thing. In trying to piece together some of the multitudinous fragments of our collective trip with him, however, I realize that I have been stalking a mythical beast. Each time I think that I have understood its nature, that I am close to killing or capturing it, it reappears in another guise, perhaps even tenfold in number.

The singular thing I conclude with certainty is that Trump is at his best when he is awful. The worse he behaves, the more attention he draws to himself, the more some people love him for it, while others condemn him. Never count him out, no matter how terrible his behavior. He is resilient and shrewd even as he reveals amazing political incompetence. Although good at playing one, he is no fool. He has masterfully cultivated his celebrity, playing on our national preference for illusion over reality. He understands hyperbole and myth making, knows how to brand himself and how to pose as a symbol of something important that may turn out to be hollow at the core. Above all, at some deep level he understands the American people's love and longing for greatness – and their fear of losing it.

My focus over these past few months, in fact, shifted from Trump himself to how his personality seems to strike such a resonant chord in so many people. Something else happened to me in Australia as I watched the young couple with the selfie stick posing before the koala bear. I was seized by the notion of Trump as an intrusive, omnipresent, and terrible-to-behold mirror image of what I think of as America's worst public face. In his bullying, aggressive, materialistic, racist, and totally unreflective poses, he is what the world must see as the worst side of America's greatness. No wonder Putin may, indeed, wish to help Trump win.

As a selfie of our own worst side, Trump is the modern incarnation of Narcissus, the Greek beauty who is oblivious to everything but himself. Trump's self-interest and grandiosity appeal to his followers in their desperate need for something grand and powerful to help them avoid confronting the phenomenon of "extinction anxiety." This is not just what Freud called the "death instinct" in individuals, but a fear that everything we care about will ultimately vanish. My work has convinced me that all of us at some level fear that "our people" – white, black, Muslim, Latino, whatever the group to which we belong – are in danger of extinction. Certainly, many people sense that America itself is threatened with extinction. Somewhere in our unconscious, if not our consciousness, we even feel that life on the planet is in danger of extinction.

Thus, my core conclusion is that there is a perfect fit between Trump's projection of largeness and greatness and the narcissistic injury to many Americans of their essential notion of who we are as a people. It was his particular, if malicious, political genius to launch his campaign with an attack on political correctness: "Get 'em outta here!" That injunction made its first appearance at his early rallies, when he urged the faithful in his crowds to get rid of protesters. It was the precursor of his pledge to rid the country of Muslims, Mexicans, and others who were portrayed as dangerous threats to the American Way of Life.

We must not underestimate what a tremendous relief it is to many people to be liberated from the handcuffs of political correctness they felt they were being forced to wear and to give vent to its nasty underbelly of racism, sexism, and hostility to others not like them. "Get 'em outta here" is Trump's promise to the faithful in protecting the country against further injury and decline. It is the foundational defensive premise of his campaign. Defend, bully, and attack – this is what Trump does best. By identifying with him, Trump's followers have found in his grandiosity the cure for their own sense of powerlessness and inferiority and the power to fight back against their own extinction. Once the enemy is expelled, they join their Maximum Leader in his righteous crusade to "Make America Great Again."

Magically, they will have found immortality – they are in the selfie with him, as is some part of all of us.

Note

1 Thomas Singer, "If Donald Trump Had a Selfie Stick, We'd All Be in the Picture," *Moyers,* August 12, 2016, https://billmoyers.com/story/donald-trump-selfie-americas-worst-side/. By permission of Judy Doctoroff, Public Square Media.

5 Op-ed pieces

I became more active in expressing political opinions as the Trump presidency careened from one debacle to the next, each further undermining the very foundations of our democracy. I began to write op-ed pieces, a few of which were published. Here is a sampling of those shorter pieces, in which I focus on the wall between Mexico and US border states, Trump's use of "fake news" as the real wall, his attacks on Senator John McCain, and finally "On Howling in Mill Valley as a Form of Walt Whitman's Barbaric Yawp" from the soul of democratic America. The first piece appeared as an op-ed piece in the New York Daily News *and the last piece appeared in* Moyers, Bill Moyers's *online journal.*

What walls symbolize: we must understand their meaning to appreciate the power of what's at the center of the shutdown

From *The New York Daily News*, January 18, 2019.[1]

Figure 5.1 President Donald Trump reviews border wall prototypes on March 13, 2018, in San Diego. (Evan Vucci/AP)

(https://aras.org/vision-folly-american-soul)

After President Trump's recently departed chief of staff, John Kelly, suggested that the border wall his former boss demands wasn't actually a wall, Senator Lindsey Graham added that the wall is merely "a metaphor for border security." All the president's men tried to "walk back" the wall, but Trump would have none of it. Perhaps that's because he knows the difference between a symbol and a metaphor, and he wanted to reaffirm the symbolic weight of the word *wall* that he has been erecting in the American psyche since 2016 (Figure 5.1).

More than a metaphor, the wall is a symbol. And, when a symbol becomes potent enough to shut down the government, we should pause to review what a symbol is and how Trump's wall operates as such. In so doing, we may better understand the furor and monumental impasse it has created.

A symbol's power lies in its polyvalency: It can evoke many simultaneous emotions and meanings, even contradictory ones. And a symbol can accrue meaning over time – for example, the American flag, the Christian cross, or the Nazi swastika – so that history adds to its gravitas. A symbol's power to move people comes from its ability to tap the depths of the human psyche, where primitive, nonrational emotions lie dormant, waiting to be roused.

Trump's wall draws part of its symbolic power from the long human history with walls. The Soviets built the Berlin Wall to keep citizens in, while the Chinese used the Great Wall to keep the Mongols out. Trump's proposed wall is intended to keep dangerous people, such as terrorists and criminals, at bay. There are also racist and ethnic currents in the motivation to build Trump's wall, as it would fulfill his campaign promise to keep "bad hombres" out of the country.

Thus Trump's wall arouses deep, highly conflicted emotions because it means different things to different people. To those who favor the wall, it taps deep yearnings for security in a world filled with perceived physical, emotional, social, and spiritual dangers. The wall promises safety, even salvation, to those who fear that multiculturalism could dilute our national purity – whatever that is.

The fact is, we are all being invaded by overwhelming forces – too much information, economic pressures, and deep fears of loss of status and privilege. All of this can be projected onto the invading horde from the south. The wall offers symbolic protection, securing our physical, social, and economic well-being.

For others, the symbolic wall activates opposite emotions. It is experienced as the deepest violation of who we are, as a people, and of those who seek a better future in the United States. It obstructs our ability to embrace immigrants who bring vitality, energy, and renewal to our multicultural society. It violates our values of freedom, difference, and goodwill for humanity. For those of us who oppose the wall, it is a symbol of tyranny, oppression, and monolithic vanity, evoking shame and outrage about what we are becoming. These conflicting meanings and emotions can be triggered simply by the mention of the single four-letter word: *wall.*

For those who hate Trump's wall, it may be well to remember that for many, including the Tibetan Buddhists who know as much about the inner spiritual world as anyone, walls can protect what is most precious and vulnerable, as in their sacred paintings (Figure 5.2).

Figure 5.2 This Tibetan tangka shows a wall protecting the sacred center

(https://aras.org/vision-folly-american-soul)

Similarly, I imagine that, for those who favor Trump's wall, it symbolizes protection of the most precious and vulnerable aspects of American life. For those who love the wall, it would be well to remember that walls – symbolic or real – can segregate, traumatize, and foment hatred and division.

It seems abundantly clear that the multiple meanings and powerful emotions of the symbolic wall have been politically manipulated and orchestrated to divide the country and literally to shut down the government. Such is the power of symbols to move people, to divide people, and to unite people in other circumstances. We are being blocked – psychically, emotionally, and legislatively – by this very potent symbol. Our leaders and we, as citizens, would do well to discuss all that the wall symbolizes. Only then might we dismantle the barriers between us to move forward as a nation.

Fake news as the real wall

Written in 2019.
        "Fake News" is the Real Wall and Trump has been building it for a Lifetime.

The daily flood of lies from the President of the United States is mind-boggling in itself, were it not for the even more astounding fact that a significant percentage of Americans embrace his lies as facts or don't care about facts at all. They accept Trump's proclamation: "The rigged and corrupt media is the enemy of the people." Underlying this phenomenon is a perfect fit between Trump's personal psyche and the group psyche of his base. What does this mean?

Trump's personal psyche seems to be based on a foundation of lying that has been the trademark of his personal narrative, which itself can be read as a chronicle of "fake news." Whether Trump's lies are strategic, sociopathic, delusional, self-aggrandizing, or a mix of all four often remains obscure. In his labeling of the mainstream news media as creators of "fake news," he projects his chronic lying onto others. Here, he performs a remarkable hat trick by turning his lies around to accuse those who disagree with him of creating "fake news." The success of this "fake news" trope lies in its ability to trigger powerful emotions that distract and divide us. What increases confusion and consternation is that so many of our fellow citizens buy Trump's sleight of hand without skepticism. They comprise the other part of this baffling equation of Trump and his followers.

What is understandable, however, is that many Americans, now called "Trump's base," feel that they have been lied to over a long period of time. Yet they eagerly embrace Trump as a truthteller. How did *this* happen? Perhaps too many false promises of a better life have, over decades, been delivered by ever-more pat-sounding politicians with a political rhetoric saturated with the catch phrases of advertising. This has raised unrealistic expectations, whose disappointments contribute to a deep distrust of career politicians and mainstream media.

This has been a bipartisan letdown. President Bill Clinton's promises of developing new industries in the Midwest through retraining workers who had endured the loss of manufacturing jobs to overseas manufacturers is an example of such failed political promises increasing suspicion of foreign trade agreements among blue-collar workers. George W. Bush and Barack Obama approved support of corporate banks "too big to fail." This has fed a growing sense among many that the expert truths of the "elites" – a group defined by technocratic expertise, access to capital, degrees from top-tier universities, and six-figure salaried jobs – are not *their* truths. Their truths point to more basic needs: to protect homes from foreclosure, to keep dying communities together, and to prevent "Them" – be they elites, immigrants, or other minorities – from taking resources away from hard-working Americans.

These conflicting sets of truths are indeed mutually exclusive: each looks like "fake news" to the other. What strains the imagination is a profound irony: The union between Trump and his base is one in which Trump, a consummate liar, is lying to his base, a group of people deeply suspicious of being lied to. And the base, in turn, believes Trump's lie that it is not he, but actually the "fake news" media, that is lying to them. This is crazy-making to those of us who do not buy into the almost mystical bond between Trump and his base. To state it another way, Trump's lifetime of lying is reflexively, habitually, and immutably projected onto others, and the mirror image is that significant portions of the US population have their own group psyche that is similarly reflexive, habitual, and impossible to change. Every day, each side collects more distorted information to reaffirm its own point of view. It is this unholy marriage that is so dangerous: Trump's personal psyche with the group psyche of so many Americans.

We might even conclude that this unholy marriage is the real wall Trump has already built, an almost impenetrable, defensive perimeter erected around himself and his followers that forms a "fake news divide." Because it is built on a foundation of scapegoating and blame, rather than one of mutual recognition and responsibility, this psychological wall allows even less passage back and forth than the real wall Trump proposes to build on America's shared border with Mexico. The sooner we come to understand that this is the real wall that Trump has built with his base, the better we may comprehend that the news developments at which we daily shake our heads in disbelief are wholly predictable. Only then can we devote our energies to the business of removing Trump from power.

Donald Trump and malevolent transformation

Written in 2019.

The continuing attacks of Donald Trump on the deceased Senator John McCain are profoundly disturbing. I would like to suggest a psychological notion that may help to understand the shockingly ugly comments coming from the president of the United States.

Harry Stack Sullivan, one of the founding giants of American psychiatry, articulated the phenomenon of "malevolent transformation" to explain what happens to some children exposed to psychological and physical abuse at critical early stages of development. *Malevolent* is defined in the *Merriam-Webster* dictionary as "1. having, showing, or arising from intense often vicious ill will, spite, or hatred and 2. productive of harm or evil."[2] And *transformation* is the process of one thing being turned into another. *Malevolent transformation*, in the way Sullivan conceived of it, describes the phenomenon in children who, in finding their needs for tenderness answered with harsh and rejecting cruelty, discover early in life that it is not safe to seek benevolence from the world. Instead, the yearning for tenderness is transformed in their psyches into a terrible weakness that needs to be renounced at all costs and replaced with toughness and meanness. Such individuals who have learned in the depths of their souls to defend themselves with "malevolent transformation" become gifted at exploiting and treating with contempt others who show such vulnerabilities.

Through the lens of "malevolent transformation," Trump's statement about McCain's war service and imprisonment turns a good man's long-suffering heroism into a weakness more reflective of Trump's own fears of vulnerability, when he says: "He's not a war hero. . . . He was a war hero because he was captured. I like people who weren't captured."[3] In fact, we might consider that many of Trump's statements about those whom he denigrates are simply a function of the psychological process of "malevolent transformation" in Trump himself. Indeed, Trump has turned the dreadful psychological experience of malevolent transformation into an art form as well as a formidable political weapon. Trump is quite gifted at turning something good into something bad while stoking hatred in others – either hatred of him or hatred in his followers for his enemies. I like to think of this as the reverse alchemical art of turning gold into shit.

What makes this all the more dangerous in a leader is that it is not only toxic in the interpersonal arena but also contagious in the public sphere. The effect of "malevolent transformation" in a leader on his followers is that they mistake the leader's contempt, envy, and cruelty for strength and courage. The infectious poison of the kind of hatred that flows from "malevolent transformation" was highlighted by the following message sent to Cindy McCain by a Trump follower within twenty-four hours of Trump's recent attacks on McCain: "Your husband was a traitorous piece of warmongering shit and I'm glad he's dead. Hope your Miss Piggy looking daughter chokes to death on the next burger she stuffs down her fat neck."[4] Malevolent transformation in individuals has devastating effects on almost everyone who come into contact with these people. Malevolent transformation in a society transforms whatever civility exists into ruthless barbarity.

"On Howling in Mill Valley as a Form of Walt Whitman's Barbaric Yawp"

From Moyers, *April 8, 2020.*[5]

Walt Whitman would be proud of the people of Mill Valley, California. Peter Reynolds, my neighbor and colleague, shows why in his video recording of the newly emerging ritual of communal howling that begins every evening at precisely 8 p.m. and which lasts for several minutes.

You can see and hear the video of Mill Valley Howling at https://tinyurl .com/ycdroccp.

The first words that came to mind when my wife and I joined in the boisterous cacophony with our fellow citizens was Whitman's phrase "barbaric yawp."

The spotted hawk swoops by and accuses me – he complains of my gab and my loitering.

> *I too am not a bit tamed, I too am untranslatable,*
> *I sound my barbaric yawp over the roofs of the world.*[6]

Whitman, considered by many to be the poet of America's soul, would recognize clearly the barbaric yawp in the chorus of hoarse and high-pitched cries in response to the "shelter in home" status imposed on all of us by the coronavirus pandemic. Over the hills and into the valleys of Mill Valley, this yawping choir rings with an uproarious thunder of clanging and hooting that is infectiously joyous and liberating. Miraculously, a broad smile erupts on our faces, even amid growing isolation and dread. The anonymous echoing and coming together of faceless voices in the night makes it all the more uncanny and powerful. That the sounds mimic the nightly howls of the local coyotes brings to mind further lines from Whitman's *Leaves of Grass*:

> I think I could turn and live with animals, they are so placid and
>   self-contain'd,
> I stand and look at them long and long.

> They do not sweat and whine about their condition,
> They do not lie awake in the dark and weep for their sins.

> They do not make me sick discussing their duty to God,
> Not one is dissatisfied, not one is demented with the mania of owning
>   things,

> Not one kneels to another, nor to his kind that lived thousands of
>   years ago,
> Not one is respectable or unhappy over the whole earth.[7]

What is a "barbaric yawp" and why do I immediately think of it when participating in the Mill Valley howling? Steven Herrmann, a friend and Jungian colleague of mine with a deep scholarly interest in Whitman, wrote the following to me years ago when I inquired about the meaning of the "barbaric yawp":

> The aim of Whitman's "barbaric yawp" was to sound a new heroic message of "Happiness," Hope, and "Nativity" over the roofs of the world, to sound a primal cry which must remain essentially "unsaid" because it rests at the core of the American soul and cannot be found in any dictionary, utterance, symbol (*Leaves*, Section #50). The "barbaric yawp" is a metaphorical utterance for something "untranslatable," a primal cry from the depths of the American Soul for the emergence of man as a spiritual human being in whom the aims of liberty and equality have been fully realized and in whom the opposites of love and violence, friendship and war, have been unified at a higher political field of order than anything we have formerly seen in America. His "yawp" is an affect state, a spiritual cry of "Joy" and "Happiness" prior to the emergence of language.[8]

Whitman would undoubtedly join in our Mill Valley howling as an expression of his barbaric yawp. TRY IT!!!!!

Notes

1 Thomas Singer, "What Walls Symbolize: We Must Understand Their Meaning to Appreciate the Power of What's at the Center of the Shutdown," *New York Daily News*, January 18, 2019, www.nydailynews.com/opinion/ny-oped-what-walls-symbolize-20190117-story.html.
2 Merriam-Webster, s.v., "Malevolent," www.merriam-webster.com/dictionary/productive.
3 Chris Cillizza, "The Awful Reality That Donald Trump's Repeated Attacks on John McCain Prove," *CNN Politics*, March 19, 2019, www.cnn.com/2019/03/19/politics/donald-trump-john-mccain-dead/index.html.
4 "Transcripts," *CNN Tonight*, March 19, 2019, http://transcripts.cnn.com/TRAN-SCRIPTS/1903/19/cnnt.01.html.
5 Thomas Singer, "On Howling in Mill Valley as a Form of Walt Whitman's Barbaric Yawp," *Moyers*, April 8, 2020, https://billmoyers.com/story/on-howling-in-mill-valley-and-walt-whitmans-barbaric-yawp/. By permission of Judy Doctoroff, Public Square Media.
6 Walt Whitman, "Song of Myself," in *Leaves of Grass*, Project Gutenberg, www.gutenberg.org/ebooks/1322.
7 Ibid.
8 Steven Herrmann, personal communication, January 2007.

6   The analyst as a citizen in the world

From the *Journal of Analytical Psychology* 64, no. 2 (2019): 206–224.[1]

In response to a call for papers for a special edition of the Journal of Analytical Psychology *on "The Analyst as Citizen in the World," I wrote this essay based on my own experience of the unfolding relationship between analysis and activism over time. It tracks the movement back and forth from an inner/individual adaptation to life to an outer/collective adaptation through the various stages in a life's journey.*

The relationship between being a Jungian analyst and a so-called citizen of the world is by no means self-evident, any more than it is self-evident what it is to be either a Jungian analyst or a citizen of the world. In fact, the only self-evident part of such a relationship is that it will inevitably be unique to each person based on temperament, typology, personal history, cultural background, and a host of other factors that make up who they are. How Andrew Samuels is an "analyst as citizen of the world" is not the same as how John Beebe or Tom Kirsch or Luigi Zoja or Joerg Rasche are "analysts as citizens of the world" or how Jules Cashford, Craig San Roque, Eva Pattis, or Anne Noonan are "analysts as citizens of the world." We wouldn't be Jungian analysts if we didn't say that each analyst must find their own way of being in the world as "analyst" and "citizen." I will describe some of what has gone into my becoming both a Jungian analyst and a citizen of the world.

As a good Jungian, I begin with a dream. In 1970, my final year of medical school, I had a dream that anticipated in the unconscious what it has taken the better part of my adult life to realize was at the heart of many of my personal and professional pursuits. Only relatively recently have

I recognized and connected with this dream as containing within it the seeds of the symbolic attitude out of which would grow my life's work in the world:

> *I am attending a United Nations session and the discussion is focused on setting up a colossal cistern or water storage facility that will sit on top of the world. Whoever needs water in the world at a given time will be determined by a computer (this was long before computers were sitting on top of the world) – so that water for the whole earth will be regulated and distributed equitably. I thought to myself, "I don't like computers very much but maybe they could do a better job distributing water fairly than politicians have done." It is a global watering hole ("whole," as I misspelled it in my dream book).*

Figure 6.1 is a drawing I made of the dream.

I hope that by the end of this essay the possible meanings of this dream and the image I made of it will become clearer in terms of my development both as a Jungian analyst and as a citizen of the world. I cite this dream in the context of Jung's notion that we are conditioned not only by the past but also by the future that gradually evolves out of us.[2] I have come to believe that this dream from my innermost depths anticipated by

Figure 6.1 Drawing of the dream from the author's dream book
(https://aras.org/vision-folly-american-soul)

decades the development of a future symbolic attitude that would take shape in specific kinds of activism that I have participated in as a citizen of the world.

The central image of the dream is the cistern, or global watering hole ("whole"). From today's perspective, a concrete as well as symbolic interpretation of the dream would make sense since in fact the world has a real and desperate need for water and its equal distribution. But, at this stage in my life, I am more focused on the symbolic meaning of the dream in terms of one's capacity to access, store, and distribute equitably the creative, life-giving energies of the individual and collective psyche of the world. In this sense, the dream can be seen as one of participating in the world soul or *anima mundi*. For me personally, connecting to and participating in the life-promoting energies that flow from the global cistern through meaningful projects in the world is where the inner and outer worlds meet.

I have divided this chapter on analysts as citizens into three interwoven parts, since I don't think you can discuss one part without placing it in the context of the other two.

- Part One: Autobiographical Reflections on the Relationship between Inner and Outer
- Part Two: A Jungian Theoretical Framework for the Relationship between Inner and Outer
- Part Three: The Rhythm of Being an Analyst and a Citizen Moving between Inner and Outer

Part one: autobiographical reflections on the relationship between inner and outer

Three major things happened to me in the mid- to late 1960s:

- I taught in Greece for a year between college and medical school and explored a different culture, its history, and way of life.
- I entered medical school, fell apart, and began a Jungian analysis and the discovery of the reality of the inner world.
- At the same time, the "outer world" was in the throes of transformation via a cultural revolution that exploded into the politics of the Vietnam War abroad and the Black Panther movement at home. The cultural revolution also turned the world of psychology and spirituality upside down in experimentation with sexuality, psychedelics, and alternative lifestyles. Many familiar attitudes and beliefs of the immediate post–World War II era gave way to what today we would lionize as "disruptive" ideas, behaviors, and beliefs.

The "outer world" of the American culture in which I had grown up and that had been firmly in place since the early 1950s was breaking apart by the late 1960s. I remember, during that time of great upheaval, returning from medical school on the East Coast to my parents' wonderfully comfortable and cultured home in St. Louis, Missouri, the heartland of the United States. I found myself watching a televised college football game that was attended by 100,000 wildly cheering people. I realized that Richard Nixon, the Vietnam War, and American football were all part of a tribalism that I no longer identified with as I began to disidentify from the national collective psychology and symbolism that Jung and his co-authors pointed to in *Man and His Symbols*.³ Both the "inner" and "outer" worlds became vividly real to me as I waded into an intensely emotional, richly symbolic, personal, and collective psychic sea. I was just sticking my toes in those waters or, more accurately perhaps, discovering that I was mostly underwater in those challenging times. In remembering that era, the *Journal of Analytical Psychology* call for these papers struck a particularly resonant chord in its statement:

> Therefore, the challenge to include precisely that part of human reality which seems to belong exclusively to the *outside world* in our psychological considerations is one of the crucial challenges we face in our work. Thus everything that is *political*, in the broadest sense of that term, can emerge and be felt as *symbolic reality*.

Robert Rauschenberg certainly understood how the outside world and everything that is political "can emerge and be felt as symbolic reality." His print, shown in Figure 6.2, vividly brings to life how the most dramatic events of the late 1960s fused into a collage not only of the outer world but something of the collective psyche that was indwelling as well.

That the inner and outer worlds simultaneously became so activated and heightened for me in their emotional intensity and imagery is one of those accidents or coincidences of biography that can determine one's fate. John Perry liked to define archetypes as affect/images, and this was a time when archetypes in the form of affect/images were knocking on everyone's door.⁵ The period between 1965 and 1970 was one of the most tumultuous and liminal in America's recent history, and it was during that time that I was studying to be a doctor. Although our country was embroiled in the most profound upheaval in the form of cultural and political "activism," I found myself drawn to the Jungian tradition and became what I have often referred to as a "baby Jungian."

If the rest of the world was in the process of going nuts, the Jungians were already there. I found this out at my first Jungian conference at Greystone Lodge in New York City in 1967, where, among others, Edward

Figure 6.2 Robert Rauschenberg, *Signs*, 1970, screenprint, 43 × 34 inches[4]
(https://aras.org/vision-folly-american-soul)

Edinger spoke about "The Secret of the Gold Flower" – or was it "The Emerald Tablets"? Whichever it was, it seemed about as far removed from what was going on in my "inner" and "outer" world as could be – and yet it was deeply attractive in a totally mysterious way. In that sense, I began to feel a profound split between the inner Jungian world that I was beginning to explore and the outer world of cultural and political turmoil in late-1960s America, which that was going haywire with its own numinous and archetypal attractions. This split crystallized dramatically for me in my memory of a day in New York City, when I first saw Fellini's *Satyricon* and stumbled out of the theatre in a transfixed daze only to find myself surrounded by a huge swirling mob of Vietnam protestors parading down Fifth Avenue. I felt truly divided and equally drawn to two very different worlds. Fifty years later, Jean Kirsch sent me an apt reference to Jung's 1916 paper "Adaptation, Individuation, Collectivity," in which the second section on "Individuation and Collectivity" begins "Individuation and collectivity are a pair of opposites, two divergent destinies."[6] Perhaps lurching out of the Fellini movie put me face to face with this pair of opposites and potential divergent destinies – the compelling richness of the inner world symbolized by Fellini's unique imagery/vision and the need for committed engagement with the outer world at a time of great national and world danger. In my own case, I ended up turning far more "inward" than "outward" by spending at least the next fifteen to twenty years in deep attentiveness to the inner world, with less and less focus on the outer world as I began my psychiatric residency and Jungian analytic training. My intense engagement with the inner world became primary. Metaphorically, I moved into Fellini's inner world of archetypal images, in which the living contents of the collective unconscious seemed to parade inside me on a nightly basis, leaving me to wander around most days trying to decipher their numinous and emotionally charged, coded messages. Certainly, the "outer" world of Vietnam and the eras of Johnson, Nixon, Carter, and Reagan caught my attention, along with other cultural and psychological movements, but somewhat in the fashion of a symbolic march of outer events that were mostly filtered or illuminated by inner contents and developments.

My focus on the inner symbolic realm became far more important to me than my life in the "outer world." It was no accident that I lived on a houseboat and had a small aquarium, in which I conducted an experiment by not using an external filter to clean the fish tank, instead observing the ecosystem develop its own filtration system of growing thick algae, dying off, and cleaning itself with a tiny, solitary eel living at the bottom of the tank – like watching the unconscious process its own material. I had the luxury of being able to cultivate a rich inner life while attending the Jung Institute as a candidate and developing a modest psychiatric practice, exploring the psychic processes of myself and my patients. I went way into the unconscious and fully believed it was the most essential reality and the only way to authentically experience the truly countercultural notion, embraced by the C. G. Jung Institute of San Francisco, that analytic training should be an inner initiatory journey with its own timing. For me, Jane Harrison's *Themis* (1927) and Joseph Henderson's *Thresholds of Initiation* (2005) became the bibles of that initiatory experience.[7]

I avidly joined the Jungian tradition with its primary focus on the inner life. The Jung who had visions of the map of Europe turning red with blood before the outbreak of World War I or the Jung who penned the controversial "Wotan" in 1936 before the outbreak of World War II was not the Jung we studied and lived in our training as analysts.[8] The Jung who was deeply tuned into the outer collective psyche became much less important than the Jung who saw individuation as differentiating out from the shadowy collective.

I think it is fair to say that after the shock of "Wotan" and "After the Catastrophe," Jung himself turned more and more to the symbolic material of the individuation process, leaving the concern with "outer" collective reality to others. Certainly, Jung was not oblivious to the "outer world," as evidenced by his writings in *Civilization in Transition*. But, as far as I know, Jungian analysts and trainees were not in the forefront of civil disobedience and protests against the war. The first and second generation of Jungians who carried on the tradition from the 1950s until the end of the twentieth century followed in Jung's footsteps for the most part, and social activism and political engagement were not a high priority. They lived and believed that "individuation" was the way to transform oneself and hopefully in, time, the world. For instance, Edinger foresaw a saving Jungian remnant emerging after the apocalypse of a world catastrophe. He believed that the postapocalyptic world would be populated by those few who had developed a consciousness grounded in depth psychology that would somehow manage to survive after the collective did itself in.[9]

There is very little in the Jungian canon from 1950 to 2000 about social and political engagement in the "outer world," except for the pioneering work of Andrew Samuels.[10] For the most part, Jungians were a small minority sect that took pride in being marginal, beyond the edges of the conventional. With its beloved esotericism almost as a badge of honor, it was easy to portray Jung's followers as being elitist, woolly headed, and mystical. I wholeheartedly joined that tradition and lived it as fully as I could, almost monastically. It was an enormous, compensatory antidote to the almost exclusively "outer" adaptation of modern mid- to late-twentieth-century American life. That one could have an inner life was a revelation at that time, and Jung was one of the notable few to bring this reality back to the modern world – even though Saint Augustine and countless others from previous eras before Jung knew it well. It wasn't as if Jung eschewed adaptation to the outer world. In the same 1916 essay I just quoted, in which individuation and collectivity were framed as a pair of opposites, Jung also wrote, "*Psychological adaptation* consists of two processes: 1. Adaptation to outer conditions. 2. Adaptation to inner conditions."[11]

By the early 1980s, my life as young Jungian had led me further and further into an inner, rather than outer, journey. Paradoxically, this intense inner journey led me outwardly to return to Greece in 1982, where I set about trying to write an autobiographical novel of a young man's strange initiatory journey that led him back to the Minoan Crete of 1500 BCE. I spent eight months writing in a tower on an isolated island bay and finally, in late October 1982, I got my main character back to this pre-Olympian time so eloquently evoked in Jane Harrison's *Themis*. It was not an easy journey, either for the main character, Isaac, or for myself. The writing became so intense and charged that I had to keep my manuscript on one side of the writing table and a journal of my almost nightly dreams about the manuscript on the other side of the table. But it was not long after getting Isaac back to Minoan Create that I realized I was at a juncture, a point of no return. I could either follow Isaac in his return to the ancient Minoan culture or return to my life and practice in the United States. I headed back to the States and left Isaac newly arrived in Minoan Crete where, to this day, he awaits my coming back to pick up his journey again. I guess you could call this an *enantiodromia*. The road I was on reversed direction completely and I began the long trip back from my profoundly introverted journey to a more worldly adaptation.

Part two: a Jungian theoretical framework for the relationship between inner and outer

When I returned from Greece in the early 1980s after my long inner sojourn, I began to take my place in the everyday outer world by falling in love, getting married, buying a house, starting a family, and building a practice as an analyst. I pretty much believed that the elders of the San Francisco Jungian tradition, Joseph Henderson, John Perry, and Jo Wheelwright, had written everything that needed to be said about human existence and there was nothing more to add. I went about the business of raising my family, witnessing the death of my parents, and working with patients.

I happen to like the theories of analytical psychology, as wobbly and patchwork as they may be, and, sometime in the late 1980s and early 1990s, I found myself wanting to work out a framework in which to understand the relationship between the world of inner development and the world of outer political and social engagement. In collaboration with then-Senator Bill Bradley, who was curious about what might be the myth of our times, I organized a small conference in Bolinas, California, that included analysts and politicians. About forty people attended, including Senator Bradley; Congresswoman Nancy Pelosi; and analysts Andrew Samuels, Clarissa Pinkola Estés, and Thomas Kirsch, among many others. In 2000, we published a book based on the conference, *The Vision Thing: Myth, Politics and Psyche in the World*.[12] The title of the book was a play on George Bush's famous quote about his problem with what he called "the vision thing," namely his lack of vision.

At the time, it occurred to me that Jungians and politicians might share a natural sense of what moved large groups of people beneath the surface of everyday events. I envisioned a potential bridge between analytical psychologists and politicians through a shared intuitive sensitivity to the movements of the collective psyche in myth, politics, and psyche. Surely politicians have a feel for what we call the collective psyche because that is their natural medium. And surely psychologists have a feel for political reality, or at least that part of it that engages the psyche. And yet, I have learned over time that the psychological and political languages, ways of thinking, and attitudes to the world are like oil and water. What appears to be a natural connection linking the two is mostly illusion when you try to talk about the psyche to politicians or politics to psychologists. Each group thinks they know what they are talking about, but neither has any real understanding of how the other truly functions. Where I imagined I would find a natural bridge was, in fact, a great chasm.

I can now see that I was especially interested in how the outer collective psyche lives inside both individuals and groups. Some might think this is sociology, but to me, that seems too extroverted a way of describing the inner living reality of the group psyche, and so I began to think of my interest and work as "inner sociology." Again, I was interested in how the outer lives in the inner and how the inner expresses itself in the outer. I wanted to frame it in the context of analytical psychology, especially in Jung's early reports of how the outer collective truly "invaded" his psyche in the form of visions and dreams before World War I and World War II. Although I was an early convert to an archetypal understanding of the psyche as a young medical student seeking to bridge spirit and nature, I had come to believe that going straight to the archetypal level to explain cultural and group phenomena (such as Jung's "Wotan") by labeling things in terms of the "hero" or the "shadow" could easily become reductionistic and neglect the deeply influential cultural and social levels of the psyche. I came to believe that an important link between the "inner" and the "outer" lay in our understanding of how culture lives inside us and how we relate to it in the outer world. This was the beginning of my attempts to contribute to the building of a theoretical bridge in the Jungian tradition between inner and outer that takes into account the personal, cultural, and archetypal levels of the psyche. In a very real sense, this was the beginning of my work on the "cultural complex" theory, which has occupied the last two decades of my professional life. I often return to Jung's early diagram (1926) of the psyche (Figure 6.3), in which he envisions various layers of the psyche as having almost geological or evolutionary strata. I find it inspirational because I think that it implicitly contains a map, not just of the inner world of the psyche but of the outer world of the psyche as well, and suggests the bridge, theoretical and practical, that I was looking for. The psyche exists in these multiple levels both in the inner and outer world.

Although some are uncomfortable with this diagram because the categories of "nations" or "large group" might be seen as opening the door to the "racial unconscious" and justifications for Nazism or any other "ism" of a large group, I do think that the psyche has a layer in it that speaks to the tendency of humans to identify themselves with larger groups based on geography, nationality, religion, ethnicity, and so on. Such a construct necessitates including contents from the cultural level of the group psyche that are distinct from both personal and archetypal contents. These "contents" live in us, and how we relate to them can determine how we relate to and act in the world.

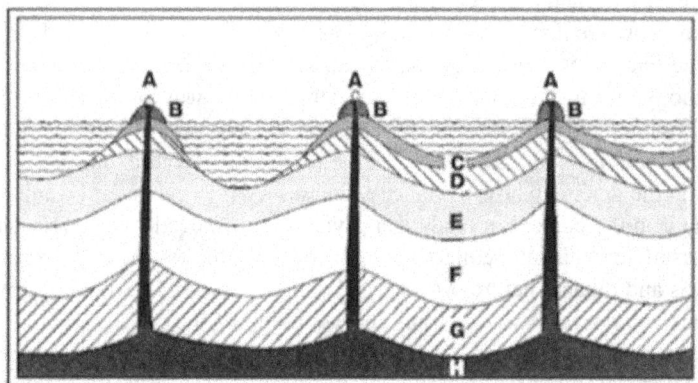

A=Individuals   E=Large group (European man for example)
B=Families   F=Primate ancestors
C=Clans   G=Animal ancestors in general
D=Nations   H="Central fire"

Figure 6.3 Jung's diagram of the psyche

(https://aras.org/vision-folly-american-soul)

Beginning with the Bolinas conference and extending to other meetings over time, I have become a good friend and colleague of Andrew Samuels, who has been the true leader of the Jungians, out of what sometimes can claustrophobically feel like the ghetto of our own tradition. Andrew abhors reified theoretical constructs and especially the often-esoteric jargon of our Jungian tradition. Andrew's brilliant and original mind was not comfortable repeating the old theoretical mantras of Jungianism. Although I find myself in sympathy with Andrew's post-Jungian contributions and especially what I like to think of fondly as his "polymorphous diversity" at every level of human activity – from the Hindu-like gods we worship to the ways in which we experience race, sexuality, and relationship – I also have felt a deep affinity for the more traditional theoretical notions of analytical psychology, especially Jung's complex theory, which has been at the heart of our San Francisco Jung Institute clinical training for close to seventy years. Perhaps unlike Andrew, I like our ramshackle Jungian theory, partly because it is not airtight or impervious to new ideas. I hold to the view that our theory retains the capacity to frame and contain contemporary perspectives and insights, even to stimulate new ways of understanding the psyche. I remain firm in the belief that the seeds of a viable Jungian psychological attitude toward the inner and outer collective life of the psyche can be the natural outgrowth of our tradition.

I use the phrase *collective psyche* to designate that part of psychic life that threads through the conscious and unconscious mind in a group of people and inside individual members of that group, whether the group be the British Society of Analytical Psychology (SAP); the San Francisco C. G. Jung Institute; or groups of white, Latino, Asian, or black people; nation-states such as the United States; or our entire global home, Earth. The collective psyche often seems to have a life of its own, and most times it is hard to define, although one can sense or intuit it in such things as the "spirit of the times." It is easy enough to confuse "collective psyche" with "sociology" in that both speak to the realities, longings, and fears that exist within various groups that differ in all sorts of significant ways: age, gender, race, socioeconomics, politics, ethnicity, culture, religious values, and so on. Sociologists describe in detail those characteristics that distinguish one group from another in "objective" categories. But how those differences actually live inside the psyche of individuals and groups is not necessarily what sociologists describe. The differences take on a more potent shape in our psyches, which do not place as high a value on "objectivity" as the sociologists of the world. One can think of the collective psyche as an *inner sociology*, a subtle thread that unites and divides and motivates people around the world and that is filled with all sorts of different group memories, affects, mythologies, and distortions about one's own group and the groups of others. Just as

Jung's great contribution to individual life was his restoring the inner world to its rightful place in the human experience, I think one of our tasks as Jungians now is to emphasize the inner reality and impact of the "collective psyche." To name the collective psyche says that there is an inner reality to the experiences of groups that gets communicated in sometimes ineffable ways that shape our deepest collective visions and fears. Most importantly, this point of view asserts that the collective psyche is part of the inner world and not just the outer world.

In this context and as part of my ongoing wrestling with the world "within" and the world "without," I found Joe Henderson's notion of the "cultural unconscious" invaluable.[13] Whereas Joe differentiated the cultural unconscious in terms of a typological model of cultural attitudes, in my collaboration with Sam Kimbles it became clear that one can think of the contents of the cultural unconscious as behaving like "complexes" in the development of the individual psyche.[14] These *cultural complexes* contribute enormously to our individual and group political and cultural attitudes and, in my opinion, form the fundamental building blocks of the cultural unconscious in the same way that Jung saw our personal complexes as fundamental to our individual psychology and the archetypes as fundamental to the collective unconscious. The basic questions of the cultural complex inquiry have been the following:

- How do contents of the cultural unconscious in the form of cultural complexes contribute to our experience of the world "within" and the world "without"?
- To what extent are cultural complexes structures of the human psyche that occur around the world and, in our curiosity about these shared structures, can we all become citizens of the world by exploring the similarities of archetypal experience and the differences of cultural complexes that are highly specific and unique to the history, geography, sociology, religion, and economics of place and people?

Asking these questions is one way that we can help analysts journey toward becoming citizens of the world.

Part three: the rhythm of being an analyst and a citizen moving between inner and outer

Few of us know the shape of our life's work or even if we will have a life's work as we set out, and often it is only retrospectively that we can tell a more or less coherent story that actually connects the inner and outer. I had such an experience in 2016 when I was invited to give a talk in Sydney,

Australia, about two projects that have engaged my energies for the past decades: the national Archives for Research into Archetypal Symbolism (ARAS) and the cultural complex research project. I had not given much thought to how the two projects might be connected. Yet, as I was considering the underlying relationship between them, the United Nations giant cistern dream from almost five decades ago, cited at the beginning of this chapter, came to mind quite spontaneously as a gift from the unconscious. As I reflected on the dream, I made what felt like a startling connection; it came almost as a revelation, between the inner dream image of the global cistern and my outer worldly professional activities of the past two decades. It felt as though there was a connection between a greater Self, symbolized by the life-giving reservoir or cistern of energies that nourishes all of us, and the planet as a whole. I began to sense that the images, affects, memories, and beliefs that form the core contents of the inner/outer world projects that have captured my imagination can all be seen as the creative waters that flow from the dream cistern that sits atop the globe. The inner big dream of decades before symbolized both an inner path of developing my relationship with life-promoting energies and an outer path represented by facilitating others' discovery and participation in those energies. The dream therefore anticipated a more activist future of connecting inner and outer, individual and collective in various professional projects.

It is in this context of making a conscious connection between a source of life-promoting energies imagined in the dream and my professional activities of the past decades that I want to mention a few of the projects that have become profoundly meaningful to me. By the linking of the inner dream cistern and the outer "water cisterns" of various collaborative projects in the world, I have discovered a feeling of belonging to the citizenship of the world. I think it would be a mistake to think that political activism is the only way to become a citizen of the world, although it is one hugely important way.

When we are fortunate enough to gain some access to the global watering "whole" cistern of the Self, creative energies can flow into the world in a variety of ways. Painters, musicians, writers, politicians, social workers, psychotherapists, gardeners, naturalists, teachers, entrepreneurs, economists, business people, or anybody who has found access to these energies can become a citizen of the world in the sense of contributing to the nourishment of the planet and all its creatures.

Before mentioning specific projects that drew me more into the world, I want to mention what I consider to be two of the essential ingredients to the realization of a meaningful connection between being an analyst and a citizen of the world: curiosity and empathy. Cultivating our instincts of curiosity about and empathy for different places and people is the natural connector between inner and outer. Montaigne, as always, said it perfectly: "There is no wish more natural than the wish to know."[15]

Where the inner and outer meet: projects of an analyst as citizen of the world

1   After practicing as an analyst in a private office for some years, I began to feel isolated and found myself wanting to become part of, and know more about, what was going on in the world outside my office. I was invited by a colleague to become a "medical expert" in the Federal Hearings and Appeals Program of the Social Security Administration, which was presided over by administrative law judges reviewing the claims of individuals seeking disability payments as a consequence of mental impairment. As a "medical expert," I was asked to give an independent assessment of disability that reflected my own opinion, not one of either the claimant or the Social Security system. I found the work fascinating and ended up serving as a medical expert for over twenty years and participating in more than one thousand hearings. I was deeply curious about the experience of the huge percentage of people with mental illness who never find their way into the office of a private therapist. In the world of Supplemental Security Income Disability Claims, I encountered just about every imaginable kind of human suffering, and some were unimaginable. Displaced and traumatized immigrants from many parts of the world, including Russia, Southeast Asia, and Latin America, stream through the system; people of color and diverse ethnic backgrounds who have not been able to find a place in the social order drift into chaos; chronic alcoholics and drug addicts appear in various stages of disintegration; people with long-standing psychosis and profound character disorders seek relief from their suffering and protection from a world that is endlessly cruel to them; and, of course, many who are trying to "game" the system claim disability as well. It always felt good to be able to sway a judge to a favorable decision for a claimant whose disability, though severe, was not readily apparent, and it didn't feel so good to find oneself over the years becoming more conservative and suspicious of the common manipulations of the system. It is a tremendous challenge to be an interpreter of what constitutes severe mental impairment, especially in the frequently adversarial conditions in which attorneys and claimants are convinced that they will not be treated fairly by the disability review process. The Social Security system of reviewing claims is complicated and involves working with many different people: judges, attorneys, claimants, clerks, and other witnesses representing different aspects of

a claim, such as vocational experts. Part of being a citizen of the world is learning to work with other citizens as a team, in a quite different way than working with individual analysands in the consulting room. Becoming a citizen of the world means participating in larger social organizations than one's own favorite professional group, although that too has its challenges.

2   I became interested in ARAS when I began to discover that the symbolic imagery occurring in dreams often had a long visual history in the imagination of humankind. The process of amplification allowed me to discover and explore the inner world of dreams in relation to the unfolding mythologies of human cultures from around the world and the beginning of time. It might seem strange to say that ARAS is a marvelous bridge between the inner world and becoming a citizen of the world, especially since ARAS was at one time one of the more esoteric Jungian hide-outs, the only way of gaining access to the paper archives being permission from a treating analyst. I had the great privilege to join others in making ARAS easily accessible to the whole world by raising the money to digitize the 18,000 images and commentary of the archives and place them on a handsome Internet site that now gets monthly visits from citizens from 135 different countries around the world. In addition, we have created *ARAS Connections*, with articles on psyche, symbol, and culture, that reaches another 10,000 people quarterly. ARAS has become a very real connector of the inner world with the outer world, as evidenced by *The Book of Symbols*, which has been translated into seven different languages and has sold 270,000 copies worldwide.[16] To me, this feels like an actual incarnation of the global watering hole (whole) dream in that we are providing access to the living waters of the depths of the psyche to fellow citizens around the world.

3   Further developing the bridge between inner and outer, between analyst and citizen, have been collaborative researches with colleagues from around the world in studying what makes our different cities and our diverse cultures unique in terms of specific histories, geographies, and cultural complexes that help define our separate identities and/ or cause us terrible conflicts at home and abroad. Cultural complex researches have stretched from Australia to Latin America to Europe to Asia to North America. It is a deep privilege and a joy to join with fellow analysts from around the world on a shared project that, to date, has engaged some eighty analysts from five continents on subjects that are deeply meaningful to all of us.[17]

4   And, as another aspect of being both analyst and citizen, it has been equally thrilling to bridge the gap between inner and outer in the present

and past by developing a series of conferences and books that explore the evolving archetypal reality of *Ancient Greece, Modern Psyche*.[18]

5   Finally, recently I have found myself in a far more direct engagement with the political realities of the US presidency. Since 2000, every four years, the C. G. Jung Institute of San Francisco has sponsored a program devoted to a discussion of the collective psyche and the current presidential election of that cycle. In 2016, we held our fifth Presidency Conference, just two weeks before the national elections when it felt as though Hillary Clinton would win, despite ominous subterranean fears that Trump might somehow upset the conventional wisdom and surprise both the nation and himself with a victory. Trump's victory led to a tsunami of anguish among a large portion of the population nationally and internationally, but the reality has been far worse than the nightmarish fears. In response to the dreadful consequences of the Trump presidency, I recently contributed to a book, *The Dangerous Case of Donald Trump*, which within the first week of its publication jumped to *The New York Times* Bestseller list, reflecting a hunger in the body politic for a psychological understanding of Trump and Trumpism.[19] It doesn't hurt that Trump is marketing our book everyday with his dangerous antics. Again, as analyst and citizen, I tried in my chapter, "Trump and the American Collective Psyche," to articulate my views as a Jungian reflecting on the collective psyche as it lives in our inner and outer worlds. Trump not only moved into the White House in 2017, he invaded the inner world of the American and global psyche, where he has taken up a chaotically dangerous residence. I believe that bringing a psychological attitude to current social and political realities is one of the more important contributions we can make as analysts who are also citizens of the world. And I think it is essential that we help make the connection for ourselves and others that our inner and outer worlds are intimately connected and interrelated in the madness that is Trumpism.

Part 4: conclusion

The publication of *The Red Book* reminded us all of the profound divide between the "spirit of the times" and the "spirit of the depths" that Jung intuited and suffered.[20] In considering the relationship between being an analyst and being a citizen of the world, I believe we are challenged to struggle with making a connection between the "spirit of the times" and the "spirit of the depths" without devaluing either one. Each "spirit" has a deep and legitimate claim on our energies and our souls. It is probably easiest to identify with one pole or the other along that spectrum, which often feels more like a split than a spectrum. Can we live in both spirits simultaneously? Can we live in the inner world and the outer world at the same time? Can we balance being both a citizen and an analyst? These questions challenge us every day and throughout the stages of our lives. I would like to think that my global watering hole (*sic* "whole") dream of close to fifty years ago has directed enough of my life, without my knowing it, to make it meaningful, and that on occasion I have found a tentative balance between being an analyst and being a citizen of the world, a balance in which the waters of each have contributed at times to a meeting between the spirit of the times and the spirit of the depths. The occasional experiences of a feeling of wholeness or individuation have come from finding myself in tune with the messages from inside and, at times, finding a way to express them in the world as a citizen. We get momentary glimpses when it all feels interconnected, but often being an analyst and a citizen of the world feels more fragmented than whole.

Notes

1 Thomas Singer, "The Analyst as a Citizen in the World," *Journal of Analytical Psychology* 64 (2019): 206–224. https://doi.org/10.1111/1468-5922.12479. © 2019 The Society of Analytical Psychology. Wiley Publishing.
2 C. G. Jung, "Analytical Psychology and Education: Three Lectures (1926)," in *The Complete Works of C. G. Jung, vol. 17, the Development of Personality* (Princeton: Princeton University Press, 1954), ¶110.
3 C. G. Jung and Marie-Louise von Franz, *Man and His Symbols* (New York: Dell, Random House, 1968).
4 See the Rauschenberg Foundation's fair use policy, www.rauschenbergfoundation.org/foundation/fair-use.
5 John W. Perry, "Emotions and Object Relations," *Journal of Analytical Psychology* 15, no. 1 (1970): 1–12.
6 C. G. Jung, "Adaptation, Individuation, Collectivity (1916)," in *The Collected Works of C. G. Jung, vol. 18, the Symbolic Life* (Princeton: Princeton University Press, 1976), ¶¶1095ff.
7 Jane E. Harrison, *Themis: A Study of the Social Origins of Greek Religion* (London: Cambridge University Press, 1927); Joseph Henderson, *Thresholds of Initiation* (Asheville, NC: Chiron Publications, 2005).
8 C. G. Jung, "Wotan (1936)," and "After the Catastrophe (1945)," in *The Collected Works of C. G. Jung, vol. 10, Civilization in Transition* (Princeton: Princeton University Press, 1968).
9 Edward Edinger, *Archetype of the Apocalypse*, ed. George Elder (Chicago: Open Court, 1999), xvi, 14.
10 Andrew Samuels, *The Political Psyche* (London: Routledge, 1993).
11 Jung, "Adaptation, Individuation, Collectivity," ¶¶1084–1106.
12 Thomas Singer, *The Vision Thing: Myth, Politics and Psyche in the World* (London: Routledge, 2000).
13 Joe Henderson, *Cultural Attitudes in Psychological Perspective* (Toronto: Inner City Books, 1993).

14 Thomas Singer and Samuel Kimbles, *The Cultural Complex: Contemporary Jungian Perspectives on Psyche and Society* (New York: Routledge, 2004).
15 Michel De Montaigne, *The Complete Essays of Montaigne, Book III* (New York: Penguin Classics, 1993), Ch. 13.
16 ARAS, *The Book of Symbols: Reflections on Archetypal Images* (Berlin: Taschen, 2000).
17 Thomas Singer, ed., *Psyche and the City: A Soul's Guide to the Modern Metropolis* (New Orleans: Spring Journal Books, 2010); Thomas Singer, *Placing Psyche: Exploring Cultural Complexes in Australia* (New Orleans: Spring Journal Books, 2011); Thomas Singer, *Listening to Latin America: Exploring Cultural Complexes in Brazil, Chile, Columbia, Mexico, Uruguay, and Venezuela* (New Orleans: Spring Journal Books, 2012); Thomas Singer and Joerg Rasche, eds., *Europe's Many Souls: Exploring Cultural Complexes and Identities* (New Orleans: Spring Journal Books); and see also *Cultural Complexes and the Soul of America* and *Spokes of the Wheel: Far East Asian Cultural Complexes*, both forthcoming from Routledge in 2020.
18 Thomas Singer and Virginia Beane Rutter, *Ancient Greece, Modern Psyche: Archetypes in the Making* (New Orleans: Spring Journal Books, 2011); Thomas Singer and Virginia Beane Rutter, *Ancient Greece, Modern Psyche: Archetypes Evolving* (London and New York: Routledge, 2015).
19 Thomas Singer, "Donald Trump and the American Collective Psyche," in *The Dangerous Case of Donald Trump*, ed. Brandy Lee (New York: St. Martin's Press, 2017).
20 C. G. Jung, *The Red Book*, ed. Sonu Shamdasani (New York and London: W. W. Norton & Co., 2009).

7   A Fool's Guide to Folly

From *When the Soul Remembers Itself: Ancient Greece, Modern Psyche*, edited by Thomas Singer, Jules Cashford, and Craig San Roque, Routledge, 2019.[1]

The onset of Trumpism in the body politic, coupled with the ongoing aging process in my own body and psyche, caused me to think more about folly and less about vision – or perhaps more about the relationship between vision and folly. Our world seems to offer many examples of the failure of vision and the prevalence of folly. At the same time, I also began to think more about how folly could be the mother of invention just as much as it is the architect of destruction. This essay is the result of my inquiry into the relationship between vision and folly, which takes us full circle back to the first essay in this book, "A Personal Meditation on Politics and the American Soul."

Part one: introduction – personal experiences with folly

A man must be a little mad if he does not want to be even more stupid.

Michel de Montaigne, Book III, Chapter XI[2]

I begin with a drawing I produced in medical school in the late 1960s (Figure 7.1). Hold it in mind as I take you on my "Fool's Guide to Folly," which starts with a few recollections of folly in my personal life. This particular drawing reflects how I have often felt in my life. It shames me a bit while also warming my heart. It depicts through the body a particular state of mind and feeling that I want to convey – the legs are disjointed in a somewhat awkward but simultaneously nimble dance. The middle part of the body is tied up obsessively in conflicting tendencies, and the head

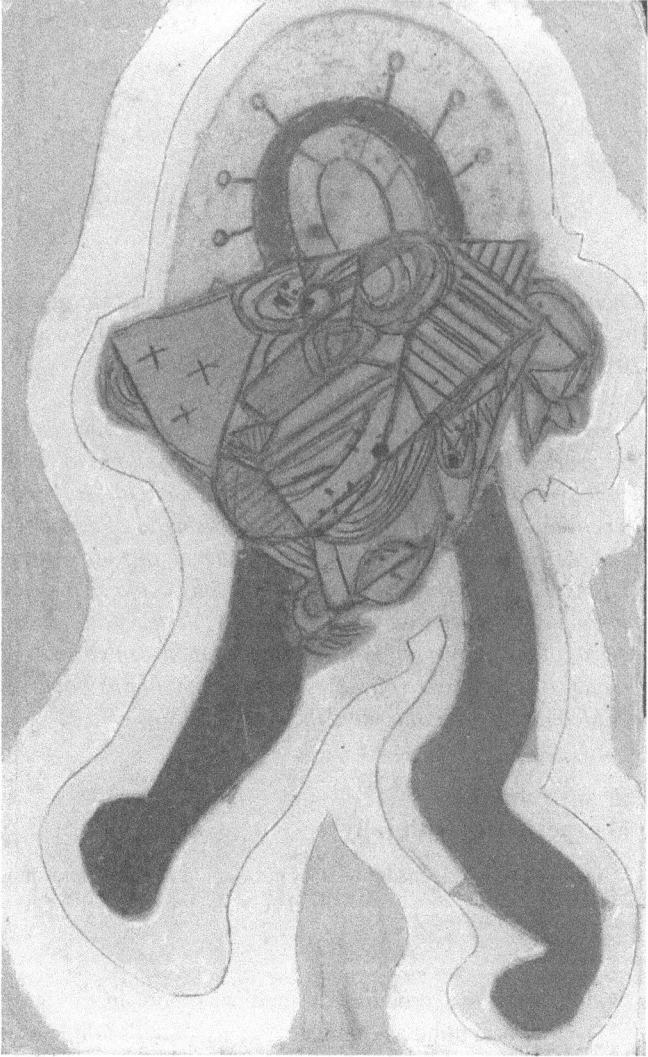

Figure 7.1 Self-portrait from medical school
(https://aras.org/vision-folly-american-soul)

has a surprisingly radiant, even illuminated, quality about it. This drawing can be seen as the self-portrait of the fool in the midst of "dancing the
folly of life."

Figure 7.2 Albrecht Dürer, *Goose Fool*, Woodcut 1511 (from www.spaightwoodgal
leries.com/Pages/Durer_Fools_1.html)

(https://aras.org/vision-folly-american-soul)

Perhaps less glowing but equally foolish is Dürer's 1511 version of the
Goose Fool (Figure 7.2), which I only recently stumbled on in writing this
essay. But he has the same knocked-kneed instability and even a hat with
a couple of doodads that bear a resemblance to the heady balls of my more
radiantly ambiguous figure – all of which reminds me of a conversation I had
with a Greek cab driver upon arriving in Athens on one of many journeys to
Greece over the decades. My pidgin Greek allowed me to engage in a simple
exchange with him. He asked me what I did and where I lived. I told him
I was a psychiatrist from the United States. He responded – with something
of his own foolish wisdom – that he was a Greek cab driver and that his
mind was much like the Aegean Sea, mostly full of watery emptiness, with
a few rocky islands interspersed. He had a sense of folly.

Here is a dictionary definition of folly:[3]

1   Lack of good sense or normal prudence and foresight. *His folly in
     thinking he could not be caught.*
2   *a* Criminally or tragically foolish actions or conduct. *b Obsolete*: EVIL,
     WICKEDNESS; *especially*: lewd behavior.
3   A foolish act or idea. *The prank was a youthful folly.*
4   An excessively costly or unprofitable undertaking. *Paying so much for
     that land was folly, since it was all rocks and scrub trees.*
5   An often extravagant picturesque building erected to suit a fanciful taste.

I maintain, however, that these definitions of folly are lacking in the more
positive and inspired variety of folly, which is generative of creativity in
life. So, there is folly and there is folly – for the source, content, and outcome of folly can often shift before one's eyes in an instant. There is the
folly that can lead one into the joyful, almost ecstatic delight in life, that
takes one on totally unexpected and essential paths, and there is the folly
that makes a mess of life or even destroys it. Sometimes these two experiences of folly are indistinguishable, sometimes one leads to the other, and
sometimes they are not linked at all. On the one hand, a sense of folly can
lead to the ability to laugh at our human foolishness, allowing us to plunge

into life with abandon, enjoying the folly of being human that occasionally joins hands with divine folly and the creative madness that it can inspire. And a sense of folly can allow us to tolerate and even laugh at what is otherwise both unbearable and ridiculous – a challenge that faces many of us today, both in the United States and in the rest of the world on a daily basis. As Jung said, "Do you believe, man of this time, that laughter is lower than worship? Where is your measure, false measurer? The sum of life decides in laughter and in worship, not your judgement."[4]

There is also that kind of absurdly blind folly that can launch major powers into reckless wars that achieve nothing but the destruction of countless lives and unending animosities and trauma that pass from generation to generation. This essay, then, foolishly presents itself as a Fool's Guide to Folly, exploring both the creative and destructive sides of folly – that which is humanly or divinely inspired and that which is blindly stupid. And there are many shades of folly in between these extremes – from the sublime to the horrific, from the comic to the tragic, from the life-affirming to the death-dealing. Folly includes everything from play to murder. Folly can be a truth teller, and folly can be a deceiver. Folly can lead us forward, and folly can take us backward. Sometimes the roles played by the fool and by folly get all mixed up with one another and we find ourselves in a stew of folly, revealing and hiding the truth of folly leading us forward and backward in human and social development. For instance, in 1867, US Secretary of State William H. Seward negotiated a treaty with Russia for the purchase of Alaska for $7 million. Despite the bargain price of roughly two cents an acre, the Alaskan purchase was ridiculed in Congress and in the press as "Seward's folly." After a slow start in US settlement, the discovery of gold in 1898 brought a rapid influx of people to the territory, and Alaska, rich in natural resources, has contributed to American prosperity ever since.

Perhaps we come to know Folly best through the emotions she (following Erasmus, who identifies her as feminine) evokes in us, which range from joy and delight, to horror and disgust, to shame and humiliation, and finally from incredulity and disbelief to their opposites of credibility and belief. Folly is polymorphous indeed.

A landmark date in my personal discovery of folly was in the summer of 1963, when I spent my first day ever in Greece by buying a copy of the newly published English version of Nikos Kazantzakis's *Zorba the Greek* and climbing Mt. Lycabettus in the heart of Athens. After the steep climb, the blinding sun, and the magic of reading *Zorba the Greek* for hours atop Lycabettus, I was never quite the same. *Zorba the Greek* is the story of a young English writer named Basil who has come to Greece to inspect an abandoned mine in Crete owned by his father. He invites Zorba to join him on his trip and "folly strikes." In many ways, Zorba himself can be seen as the very incarnation of divinely inspired human folly, as can be seen in "The Full Catastrophe," a scene in which Zorba tells Basil, "Am I not a man? And is a man not stupid? I'm a man, so I married. Wife, children, house, everything. The full catastrophe" (Figure 7.3).[5]

Figure 7.3 Film Clip: *Zorba the Greek*, "The Full Catastrophe" (https://aras.org/vision-folly-american-soul)

Perhaps the height of Zorba's folly – and his message of folly to the Boss (Basil) – comes in the wonderful misadventure of a lumbering scheme that includes building a contraption to carry logs from a mountaintop to the sea (Figure 7.4).

Figure 7.4 Film Clip: *Zorba the Greek*, "The Collapse of the Structure" (https://aras.org/vision-folly-american-soul)

This is the kind of inspired folly that ends in literal collapse and disaster, but not in the breaking of the human spirit. Throwing oneself into life with a sense of folly can be liberating and affirming of the human (and perhaps the divine) spirit. It is the affirmation of plunging into life itself, not unlike Joseph Conrad's advice, spoken by the German Stein, in *Lord Jim*:

> The shadow prowling amongst the graves of butterflies laughed boisterously.
> "Yes! Very funny this terrible thing is. A man that is born falls into a dream like a man who falls into the sea. If he tries to climb out into the air as inexperienced people endeavour to do, he drowns – *nicht wahr?* . . . No! I tell you! The way is to the destructive element submit yourself, and with the exertions of your hands and feet in the water make the deep, deep sea keep you up. So if you ask me – how to be?"
> His voice leaped up extraordinarily strong, as though away there in the dusk he had been inspired by some whisper of knowledge. "I will tell you! For that, too, there is only one way."
> With a hasty swish of his slippers he loomed up in the ring of faint light, and suddenly appeared in the bright circle of the lamp. His extended hand aimed at my breast like a pistol; his deep-set eyes seemed to pierce through me, but his twitching lips uttered no word, and the austere exaltation of a certitude seen in the dusk vanished from his face. The hand that had been pointing at my breast fell, and by-and-by, coming a step nearer, he laid it gently on my shoulder. There were

things, he said mournfully, that perhaps could never be told, only he had lived so much alone that sometimes he forgot – he forgot. The light had destroyed the assurance which had inspired him in the distant shadows. He sat down and, with both elbows on the desk, rubbed his forehead. "And yet it is true it is true. In the destructive element immerse." . . . He spoke in a subdued tone, without looking at me, one hand on each side of his face. "That was the way. To follow the dream, and again to follow the dream – and so – *ewig-usque ad finem*. . . ." The whisper of his conviction seemed to open before me a vast and uncertain expanse, as of a crepuscular horizon on a plain at dawn – or was it, perchance, at the coming of the night?[6]

I remember reading and studying *Lord Jim* as an adolescent and, just as Zorba's "full catastrophe" took up permanent residence in my soul, so did the phrase "in the destructive element immerse."

This is the positive notion of folly into which the Zorbatic spirit initiated me. Feeling much like the bookish narrator, I began my own dance with Zorba and his joyful embrace of folly, of setting reason aside for a different kind of logic that can affirm the nonrational as a source of life. Retrospectively, I have come to think of this kind of folly as a kind of inspired madness that just a few years later allowed me to jump into a crazy project with some friends and plant our little flag on a remote, empty bay named Klima, some ten miles from Santorini, where, in time, we built three houses. The Klima folly has continued for almost fifty years, although we are running out of juice and inspiration.

Figure 7.5 The dock that lasted twenty-four hours at Klima

(https://aras.org/vision-folly-american-soul)

In the spirt of Zorba's doomed construction project, our most glorious failure at Klima (other than starting the project at all and not knowing what to do about it now, as we age) was building a 30,000-pound cement dock that lasted less than twenty-four hours (Figure 7.5). The cement had not hardened when a huge spring storm swept the entire baby dock into the Aegean. It was our own moment of the Zorbatic falling apart of the grand scheme.

I remember another moment of being possessed by the spirit of folly, which long has been a source of embarrassment about how crazy I was in medical school but which, in retrospect, had its own wisdom. I was attending medical school in New Haven in the late 1960s. As one can glean from Robert Rauschenberg's *Signs*, it was, among other things, a time of great political and cultural upheaval, of overwhelming and highly charged folly – all mixed up in a psychic stew that one swam in, sometimes just hoping not to drown, other times delighting in its thrilling and unexpected highs, and ultimately witnessing the devastation that flowed from its folly (Figure 7.6).

Figure 7.6 Robert Rauschenberg, *Signs*, 1970 silkscreen

(https://aras.org/vision-folly-american-soul)

I vividly remember the violent outbreak of riots in New Haven in 1970, when I found myself literally in the middle of it as a volunteer first aid and crowd control person. Bobby Seale, a famous leader of the Black Panthers, was on trial in New Haven for murdering an informant. It was a chaotic and disorienting time, with black rage flaring at home and the war in Vietnam raging abroad. One day, while on a pediatric clerkship, I showed up for rounds with a child's holster strapped around my head like a hippie bandana, with the toy guns hanging over each of my ears. When asked what in heaven's name I was doing appearing on the ward like that, I answered, "I can't hear you. I have guns in my ears." I'm very lucky they didn't throw me out of medical school and commit me to the psychiatric wards. I was quite mad, but in some ways, I was acting out a frightening truth for all of us.

To introduce the tour through this history of the different kinds of folly and fools that have captured the human imagination and spirit over time, I have included a link to a three-second film image from Fellini's *Satyricon*, of visitors being shuttled through a museum. Perhaps we can metaphorically think of ourselves as being like these tourists in *Satyricon* who roll by in the background of this scene as we take a brief tour of the ancient, medieval, and contemporary museum of folly (Figure 7.7).[7]

Figure 7.7 Film Clip: museum tour in *Satyricon*

(https://aras.org/vision-folly-american-soul)

Part two: Plato's Cave

> There is no wish more natural than the wish to know.
> Michel de Montaigne, Book III, Ch. XIII[8]

What better place to start our Fool's Guide to Folly than in Plato's Cave, which appears in Plato's *The Republic*, written somewhere between 380 and 360 BCE in the Classical Age of Greece.

The Cave marks a beginning of the awakening in the history of the Western psyche of a split between the real and the illusory. What we take to be

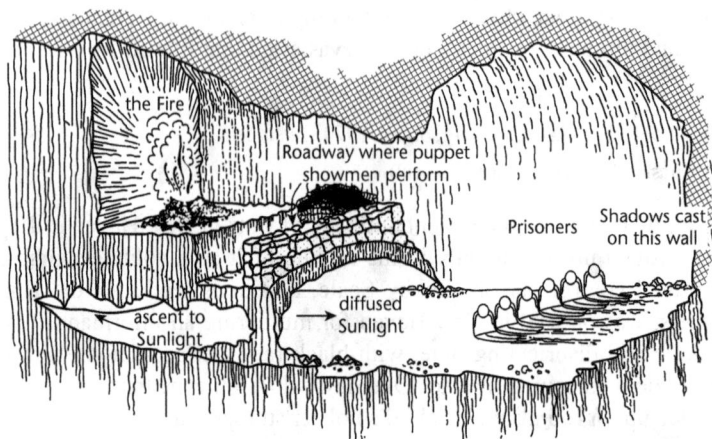

Figure 7.8 Plato's Cave

(https://aras.org/vision-folly-american-soul)

real in the everyday world may, at best, be a shadowy illusion of reality, which in fact is truly known only in the realm of ideal forms, of which Jung's archetypes would be an expression.

Here is a wonderful image of the Cave that orients us to the central features of Plato's allegory (Figure 7.8).[9]

Imprisonment in the cave

Human beings, known as "prisoners," are lined up facing a wall on which they see shadows dancing before their eyes. Puppeteers carry objects on a roadway behind the backs of the prisoners. Behind the roadway is a fire. The fire's light casts shadows of the puppeteer's objects onto the wall that the prisoners are facing. What we see as mortals, according to Plato, are the shadows of objects, not the real thing. And even the objects themselves do not reflect reality. To perceive the true forms of reality, one needs to leave the cave altogether and emerge into the light of the "real world" embodied in the "sunlight" (which was a bit how I felt when I climbed Lycabettus as a young man and began to read *Zorba the Greek* in the full, dazzling light of the Greek summer sun).

Departure from the cave

Plato asks us to imagine that a prisoner is freed to turn around and is blinded by the light of the fire, which is actually the source of light casting the reflected shadowy images onto the walls at which the prisoners gaze. The prisoner would have to decide what is real and what is shadow, and Plato imagines that the freed prisoner would turn away and run back to what he is accustomed to (that is, the shadows of the objects). Plato writes "it would hurt his eyes, and he would escape by turning away to the things which he was able to look at, and these he would believe to be clearer than what was being shown to him."[10] Plato continues his narrative:

> Suppose . . . that someone should drag him . . . by force, up the rough ascent, the steep way up, and never stop until he could drag him out into the light of the sun. The prisoner would be angry and in pain, and this would only worsen when the radiant light of the sun overwhelms his eyes and blinds him.
>
> Slowly, his eyes adjust to the light of the sun. First he can only see shadows. Gradually he can see the reflections of people and things in water and then later see the people and things themselves. Eventually, he is able to look at the stars and moon at night until finally he can look upon the sun itself (516a). Only after he can look straight at the sun "is he able to reason about it" and what it is (516b).[11]

Return to the cave

Plato imagines that the freed prisoner would think that the world outside the Cave was superior to the world he experienced in the Cave; "he would bless himself for the change, and pity [the other prisoners]" and would want to bring his fellow cave-dwellers out of the cave and into the sunlight (516c).[12]

The returning prisoner, whose eyes have become accustomed to the sunlight, would be blind when he reenters the Cave, just as he was when he was first exposed to the sun (516e).[13] According to Plato, the prisoners would infer from the returning man's blindness that the journey out of the Cave had harmed him and that they should not undertake a similar journey. Plato concludes that the prisoners, if they were able, would therefore reach out and kill anyone who attempted to drag them out of the Cave (517a).[14]

If we accept Plato's allegory of the Cave as an accurate reflection of something about the human condition, we can begin to imagine the various places in the Cave, or stages in the unfolding of the story, in which both the fool and folly might take up permanent but shape-shifting residence and play a role in the story's evolution. Here are folly's potential places or roles in the Cave that I have imagined; the reader may come up with more.

- *Folly of everyday life*, otherwise known as stupidity, can be quite destructive in its refusal to see anything other than the reflected images on the wall as being real. This is the fate of most "prisoners." And, if we imagine Folly as a god or goddess (which we will see Erasmus doing almost two thousand years after Plato), there is ample room for her to play huge tricks on us with the objects she parades in front of the fire to reflect on the wall as shadowy images – including images of ourselves.

• An enormous human *creative* (perhaps divinely inspired) *folly* is needed to step outside the cave in the first place, even if the prisoner is initially dragged out.

• The prisoner who has stepped outside the cave needs *divine folly* to compassionately reenter the cave in an effort to awaken the prisoners who will laugh at the fool who stepped outside; doubt his story of what exists outside the cave; and, perhaps, as Plato tells the story, kill the fool for presenting another view of reality that throws their own illusory view of what's real into doubt.

We might think of these follies as a tripartite or quadrated theory of folly that emerges out of Plato's primal split of the Western psyche into an illusory world of everyday reality and the real world of ideal forms:

• The totally ignorant, stupid form of folly, in which we are unable to see anything but shadowy reflections of objects floating in front of us that we take to be absolutely real.

• A divinely inspired human madness form of folly that allows us to step out of the cave in the first place and glimpse the world of Pure Forms, what Jungians have come to know as archetypes – which can be just as deceiving if taken too literally as concrete reality.

• A compassionate form of folly that would lead us back into the cave with the misguided notion that the prisoners inhabiting it would want to be awakened from their illusory world.

• A tricksterish form of Folly that would insert herself in the role of puppeteer, showing the prisoners images that would simply reflect back to them the way in which they would like to see themselves and the world. (Erasmus will have more to teach us about this incarnation of Folly.)

In this chapter, I hope to show you the many forms that folly can take as I have extrapolated them from an imaginal excursion into Plato's Cave with both the Fool and Folly as my guide. But should we take Plato too seriously, Aristophanes was already on the scene in his play *The Clouds*, referring to Socrates and his school as the "Thinkery," where the folly of fools was being pursued in such important questions as the origin of the humming sound of gnats:

> Our Chaerephon was asking [Socrates'] opinion/on whether gnats produce their humming sound/by blowing through the mouth or through the rump.
>
> (ll. 156–158)

> [Socrates] said the gnat has a very narrow gut,/and, since the gut's so tiny, the air comes through/quite violently on its way to the little rump;/ then, being an orifice attached to a narrow tube,/the asshole makes a blast from the force of air.
>
> (ll. 160–164)[15]

Part three: Erasmus's *The Praise of Folly*

> Whoever will be cured of ignorance, let him confess it.
>
> Michel de Montaigne[16]

Plato wrote his allegory of the cave between 380 and 360 BCE. Some 1800 years later, in 1509, Erasmus conceived of *The Praise of Folly* while riding over the Alps on a horse. The book was printed in 1511.

But Erasmus was not as distant from Plato in his thought as he was in time. Plato's Cave provided Erasmus and Western humans with the template of an archetypal split between illusion (our natural condition) and reality, of mistaking shadowy reflections for what is truly *real*. This split creates fertile soil in which Folly can romp. Folly loves the split between illusion and reality. It is her natural playground, in which one minute the Fool and Folly are a source of staggering stupidity, hypocrisy, and corruption. And in the very next minute, as occurs in Erasmus's book, Folly can be a way to wisdom. In one moment, Folly cruelly caters to self-serving and destructive interests, and in the next, she points to redemption.

As I mentioned earlier, if we put ourselves in Plato's Cave and imagine where Erasmus's Folly would be working her magic, she would most likely spend much of her time on the "roadway where puppet showmen perform" (as labeled in the drawing of Plato's Cave). Indeed, she may be the star "puppet showman" on that stage, in which objects destined to become shadowy reflections on the wall of the Cave are paraded in front of the fire. In Erasmus's *The Praise of Folly*, Folly reveals herself to be the progenitor and sustainer of the illusions that shield us from the painful truths about ourselves, others, and the world as a whole. She allows us to live in illusion, even as in *The Praise of Folly* she unveils her "trickery" to us as if she is encouraging us to leave the Cave. In other words, living in Plato's Cave can be thought of as akin to living in the embrace of Erasmus's Folly. What has Folly kept hidden from us in the Cave? Listen to her own voice as she reveals her sorcery to an assembly of the learned:

> What part of life is not sad, unpleasant, graceless, flat, and burdensome, unless you have pleasure added to it, that is, a seasoning of folly.[17]

In the first part of *The Praise of Folly*, Folly takes a developmental approach to her role in the lifecycle:

- About the newborn and childhood, Erasmus says through Folly:

> Who does not know that the earliest period of a man's life is by far the happiest for him and by far the most pleasant for all about him? What is it in children that we should kiss them the way we do, and cuddle them, and fondle them – so that even an enemy would give aid to one of that age – except this enchantment of folly, which prudent nature carefully bestows on the newly born; so that by this pleasure, as a sort of prepayment, they win the favor of their nurses and parents and make these forget the pains of bringing them up.[18]

- About youth after childhood, Erasmus continues through Folly:

> After childhood, comes youth. How welcome it is in every home! How well everyone wishes it! How studiously does everyone promote it, how officiously they lend it the helping hand! But, I ask, whence comes this grace of youth? Whence but from me (Folly), by whose favor the young know so little – and how lightly worn is that little! And presently when lads grown larger begin, through experience and discipline, to have some smack of manhood [aside: Erasmus did not give much thought to girls and women], I am a liar if by the same token the brightness of their beauty does not fade, their quickness diminish, their wit lose its edge, their vigor slacken. The farther one gets from me, then the less and less he lives, until *molesta senectus* (that is, irksome old age) arrives, hateful to others, to be sure, but also and more so to itself.[19]

- And about old age, Folly proclaims:

> Old age would not be tolerable to any mortal at all, were it not that I, out of pity for its troubles, stand once more at its right hand; and

just as the gods of the poets customarily save, by some metamorphosis or other, those who are dying, in like manner, I bring those who have one foot in the grave back to their infancy again, for as long as possible; so that the folk are not far off in speaking of them as "in their second childhood." (Figure 7.9)[20]

Figure 7.9 David Hockney, *Ann at a Mirror Combing*, 1979 (www.pinterest.com/pin/242420392418506876/)

(https://aras.org/vision-folly-american-soul)

If anyone would like to know the method of bringing about this alteration, I shall not conceal it. I lead them to my spring of Lethe – for that stream rises in the Fortunate Isles, and only a little rivulet of it flows in the underworld – so that then and there they may drink draughts of forgetfulness. With their cares of mind purged away, by gentle stages they become young again. But now, you say, they merely dote, and play the fool. Yes, quite so. But precisely this it is to renew one's infancy. Is to be childish anything other than to dote and play the fool? As if in that age the greatest joy were not this, that one knows nothing!!!![21]

Folly is the one thing that makes fleeting youth linger and keeps ugly old age away.[22]

For Erasmus, Folly, then, is the source of illusions and only illusions make life bearable. Folly tricks everyone into seeing nonexistent good qualities in themselves and others. Her magic enables husbands to tolerate wives, wives to tolerate husbands, and teachers to tolerate students and vice versa. Without folly no one could bear his or her companions, to say nothing of him- or herself.

Folly especially turns on those who supposedly embody wisdom and piety. In the second section of *The Praise of Folly*, she turns her sardonic wit on and exposes the hollowness of most humans – especially merchants and those who make claims to authority or wisdom. This includes grammarians, poets, rhetoricians, authors, lawyers, logicians, theologians, scientists, monks, priests, kings, courtiers, bishops, cardinals, popes, and all those who make claim to wisdom. I'm afraid a modern version of these professions would likely include myself and most of my dear readers. Erasmus's contemporary, Sebastian Brant, enumerated some 112 different kinds of fools in his 1494 book *Ship of Fools*, which, interestingly enough, also originated in an allegory from Plato's *The Republic* (Figure 7.10).

Figure 7.10 Albrecht Dürer in *Stultifera navis* (*Ship of Fools*) by Sebastian Brant, published by Johann Bergmann von Olpe (de) in Basel in 1498

(https://aras.org/vision-folly-american-soul)

In the third part of *The Praise of Folly*, the role of Folly dramatically shifts and takes on a far more positively transformative aspect in Erasmus's cosmology. In this section, Erasmus, a devout Christian – although he is highly critical of the Christianity of his time – praises the Folly that leads man to a true Christian life. Here is how Anthony Grafton writes about this Folly in his Foreword to the Princeton classic edition:

> In the third and shortest part of her speech, Folly pivots again – this time to the teaching of Christianity and philosophy. What looks to humans like wisdom, she argues, is really madness. . . . True Christianity, Folly argues, yields none of the things that ordinary, prudent men and women seek: not wealth, not power, not fame. Instead, it offers "the foolishness of the cross" by which Jesus brought healing to sinful humanity. . . . True Philosophy, Folly argues, is not a pursuit of useless knowledge or sophisticated logical tricks, but a "study of death," in Plato's words, "because it leads the mind away from visible and bodily things, and certainly death does the same." True Christianity and true philosophy converge. Both teach those who embrace them to be fools to this world, "rapt away in the contemplation of things unseen."[23]

As you can see, with Erasmus we find ourselves once again in Plato's Cave, out of which Folly is encouraging us to emerge into the light. What a Fool's Guide to Folly both Plato and Erasmus offer us!

Part four: the Wise Fool in Shakespeare's *King Lear* by Jules Cashford

The Wise Fool has two virtues: the gift of seeing through appearances to the reality within them and the ability to *play* the fool, to show the real folly its "form and pressure."

In Plato's terms, perhaps the Wise Fool, embodying divine folly, might be seen as the one who has been freed from the Cave but returns out of compassion to free the other prisoners. His wisdom is to understand that the "real folly" is the blindness of those in the Cave, which means they will not be able to accept the truth presented to them as fact until they have let go of their conviction that what they see is real. Thus, the Wise Fool has to play with the ideas of those still imprisoned so that they might begin to laugh at, and then call into question, what they are seeing – even though it is all they can see, strapped as they are to their seats before the screen. This form of *divine* folly is designed to prevent human folly from making sense and so eventually to free the prisoners from illusion. This prison is ultimately Plato's symbol of the "unexamined life."

Shakespeare's response to this in his play *King Lear* is to show, through the fates of Lear and Gloucester, that we cannot see truly unless we "see feelingly," which is to see with our whole being. From the moment the play begins, it is clear there is division in the kingdom and, ultimately, within the King himself, because he sees people without feeling – only as reflections of himself. Lear proposes to give his kingdom to his three daughters in equal parts, but asks instead for them to give something to him – to earn their portion of his "gift" by telling him how much they love him and even, in an elision of love and land, to compete for territory with flattery:

> Which of you shall we say doth love us most,
> That we our largest bounty may extend
> Where nature doth with merit challenge?
> > (Act I, scene i, lines 31–33)

The two elder sisters, Goneril and Regan, reply in kind. Lear turns to his favorite, his "joy":

> What can you say to draw
> A third more opulent than your sisters?

CORDELIA: Nothing, my Lord.
LEAR: Nothing?
CORDELIA: Nothing.
LEAR: Nothing will come of nothing. Speak again.
CORDELIA: Unhappy that I am, I cannot heave
My heart into my mouth. I love your majesty
According to my bond. No more nor less.
> > (I, i, 86–93)

LEAR: So young and so untender?
CORDELIA: So young, my lord, and true.
> > (I, i, 107–108)

The play explores the essential conflict of values between them. Lear's first response is to banish her:

LEAR: Hence and avoid my sight!
> > (I, i, 124)

But later, still not getting his own way, he disowns her:

LEAR: We have no such daughter, nor shall ever see that face of hers again . . .
(I, i, 264–265)

Lear does not know he is a fool in the sense of *Ate*, the Greek goddess of Folly and Ruin, daughter of *Eris*, Strife – often called a "blind fool." The underlying metaphor in *King Lear* is one of vision and moral blindness.

But his Fool is always with him in his folly: *Lear:* "Where's my Fool? Ho, I think the whole world's asleep" (I, iv, 47). The Fool, very much awake, offers Lear a compassionately bitter wit, issuing elliptically, in allusion, analogy, and epigram, which breaks through into Lear's consciousness where reasoned argument would fail. The Fool continually taunts Lear with his judgment, to force him to grasp that he has a false notion of himself. As the Fool puts it: "Truth's a dog must to kennel" (I, iv, 120). By teasing and parodying him, the Fool prevents him from forgetting what he has done and inexorably presses him to see he was wrong: "Why, this fellow has banished two on's daughters, and did the third a blessing against his will" (I, iv, 101–104). We learn that the Fool "hath much pined away" since Cordelia went to France, and he carries Lear's deeply buried conscience as intuitive knowledge until Lear is reconciled with Cordelia – his heart, the *Cor* of Cordelia.

The Fool plays with the terms already present in Lear's mind, like a thought that will not go away, but twists them to mean the opposite of what Lear would have them mean. The fateful "nothing" always comes up:

FOOL: Can you make no use of nothing, Nuncle?
LEAR: Why, no, boy. Nothing can be made out of nothing.
FOOL: Prithee tell him; so much the rent of his land comes to.
    He will not believe a fool . . .
LEAR: Dost thou call me fool, boy?
FOOL: All other titles thou hast given away; that thou wast born with.
(I, iv, 146–147)

Then he tries it from another angle:

FOOL: Prithee, Nuncle, keep a schoolmaster that can teach thy fool to lie.
LEAR: And you lie, sirrah, we'll have you whipped.
FOOL: I marvel what kin thou and thy daughters are. They'll have me
    whipped for speaking true; thou'lt have me whipped for lying; and

sometimes I am whipped for holding my peace. I had rather be any
kind of thing than a fool. And yet I would not be thee, Nuncle. Thou
hast pared thy wit o'both sides and left nothing i'the middle.

(I, iv, 178–184)

As Lear is watchful of Goneril's frown, the Fool concludes:

Now thou art an O without a figure. I am better than thou art now;
I am a fool; thou art nothing.

(I, iv, 189–190)

And when Lear, raging at Goneril's censure of him, cries

Does any here know me? This is not Lear.
Does Lear walk thus, speak thus? Where are his eyes? . . .
Who is it that can tell me who I am?
"Lear's shadow," The Fool replies.

(I, iv, 222–227)

So crucial is the Fool to the finding of Lear's humanity that he leads Lear to
his first moment of compassion, first toward himself and then to all dispos-
sessed people.

"O Fool, I shall go mad!" (II, iv, 281). The turning point comes
when Lear hurls himself into the storm onto the heath at night – "Blow,
winds, and crack your cheeks!" (III, ii, 1) – and has to confront what
he later calls the "tempest in my mind" (III, iv, 12): Only the Fool is
with him, who, we hear, "labours to out-jest/His heart struck injuries"
(III, i, 15–16).

When Kent, in disguise, finds a hovel for them, Lear shows his first
moment of concern for another person, significantly for his Fool:

Come on, my boy. How dost my boy? Art cold?
I am cold myself. Where is this straw, my fellow?
The art of our necessities is strange
And can make vile things precious. Come, your hovel.
Poor fool and knave, I have one part in my heart
That's sorry yet for thee.

(III, ii, 68–73)

Lear makes the Fool go into the hovel before him: "In boy; go first. – You
houseless poverty" (III, iv, 27). This act of feeling moves his heart beyond

self-pity to genuine pity for others, who, now like himself, have nothing to shield them from the storm:

> Poor naked wretches, whereso'er you are,
> That bide the pelting of this pitiless storm,
> How shall your houseless heads and unfed sides,
> Your loop'd and window'd raggedness, defend you
> From seasons such as these? O! I have ta'en
> Too little care of this. Take physic, Pomp;
> Expose thyself to feel what wretches feel.
>
> (III, iv, 28–34)

Once Lear is on his way to Cordelia at Dover, the Fool disappears – as though Lear has absorbed his wisdom in his own heart. At the end, holding Cordelia's body, Lear says: "And my poor fool is hanged," bringing the Fool together with Cordelia in death.

We see this when, just before Cordelia awakens him, Lear says to the blind Gloucester:

> If thou wilt weep my fortunes, take my eyes.
> I know thee well enough; thy name is Gloucester.
> Thou must be patient; we came crying hither.
> Thou knowest the first time that we smell the air
> We wawl and cry. I will preach to thee – Mark! . . .
> When we are born we cry that we are come
> To this great stage of fools.
>
> (IV, vi, 177–184)

Lear has found his conscience and compassion, showing us the meaning of Plato's phrase: "To know you are a fool is the beginning of wisdom."

Part five: folly in modern times – Fellini and Lapham

> We are all blockheads.
>
> Michel de Montaigne

Following Plato's and Erasmus's lead over the past 2,500 years of human history, what does our polymorphous Fool and Folly look like in the modern world? (Perhaps the reader should take a break now and go throw up.) As I was imagining this section and, since we live in an era of images,

I kept coming back to scenes from Fellini's films. It occurred to me that it might work to shift from word to image and let Fellini pick up where he left us off in the museum of *Satyricon* and resume as our tour guide through the modern museum of Folly. I think Fellini must have been married to Folly, because she is truly the guiding and enlivening Spirit of so many of his films.

Let's start with the folly of everyday life – at the family dinner table in *Amarcord*, a semi-autobiographical film about a young boy growing up in an eccentric town in Fascist Italy.[24] In the clip (Figure 7.11), hilarious slapstick prevails as the folly of husband and wife plays itself out while the grandfather excuses himself to fart in another room.

Figure 7.11 Film Clip: *Amarcord*, "Dinner"

(https://aras.org/vision-folly-american-soul)

And, along with Erasmus, let's look at youthful folly as it encounters the folly of established traditions in the ritual of Catholic confession (Figure 7.12).

Figure 7.12 Film Clip: *Amarcord*, "Youthful Confession"

(https://aras.org/vision-folly-american-soul)

And then there is the folly of madness itself and even its insane wisdom in another scene from *Amarcord*, in which the family takes Uncle Teo, confined to an insane asylum, out to the country for the day (Figure 7.13). Teo climbs a tree, shouting "I want a woman!" and throws rocks at anyone who tries to get him down. When the midget nun from the asylum finally gets Teo to come down, the doctor pronounces, "Some days he's normal; some days he's not, just like the rest of us."

Figure 7.13 Film Clip: *Amarcord*, "I Want a Woman"

(https://aras.org/vision-folly-american-soul)

Just as a youth suffers the folly of institutionalized religion in the "Youthful Confession" scene in *Amarcord*, Fellini shows us that another version of Folly can also lead us out of the "caves" of religious dogma in which we are prisoners, even martyrs, into another realm of being and perhaps even joyful delight, in his film *Juliet of the Spirits*. The Grandfather as Wise Fool liberates Juliet from the cruel martyrdom of her youthful Catholicism (Figure 7.14).

Figure 7.14 Film Clip: *Juliet of the Spirits*, "Release from the Cross"

(https://aras.org/vision-folly-american-soul)

And later in the film, the Grandfather appears once again as an almost-divine incarnation of that form of Folly that is on the side of life as he leads Juliet and the beautiful Circus Queen in a joyful flight that soars away from and above the conventional attitude of the vengeful and naysaying clergyman (Figure 7.15).

Figure 7.15 Film Clip: *Juliet of the Spirits*, "The Magical Flight of Folly" (https://aras.org/vision-folly-american-soul)

If Fellini's folly-filled visions bring such joyful delight to us, other visions of modern folly are far darker. Lewis Lapham, a distinguished American essayist, recently published a book about our contemporary world entitled *Age of Folly*. Here he describes one of the many follies of our times, which gained momentum after the fall of the Berlin Wall and the breakup of the Soviet Union, when the United States was riding high:

> Reinforced by the fortunes accruing to . . . Silicon Valley . . . and by the . . . speculation floating the Dow Jones Industrial Average across the frontier of a new millennium, the delusions of omnipotent omniscience bubbled upward to so condescending a height that in March 2001, six months before the destruction of the World Trade Center, *Time Magazine* gave voice to what . . . had become a matter of simple truth and common knowledge:

> America is no mere international citizen. It is the dominant Power in the world, more dominant than any since Rome. . . .

> The old Greeks . . . had a word, hubris, for the unbridled vanity that goeth before a fall, men tempted to play at being gods and drawn to the flame of their destruction on the wings of braggart moths. Thus President George W. Bush . . . on May 1, 2003, six weeks after launching a second American invasion of Iraq, stepping aboard the aircraft carrier U.S.S. *Abraham Lincoln* . . . stationed close inshore the coast of California to pose for the news cameras under a banner headlined MISSION ACCOMPLISHED.

> . . . Boy wonder as deus ex machina in *Top Gun* navy fighter pilot costume. But what was the mission to which the banner headlined referred? . . . The accomplishment was the dramatic significance of the invasion as prime-time television spectacle. Frivolity unbound. An act of folly more glorious than any since the Athenians in 415 BC sent a costly fleet of gilded ships to its destruction in Sicily, and by so doing lost both the Peloponnesian war and the life of their democracy.[25]

George Bush's declaration of "Mission Accomplished" aboard the U.S.S. *Abraham Lincoln* might remind us of Dürer's image of the *Ship of Fools* (Figure 7.16).

Figure 7.16 Albrecht Dürer in *Ship of Fools* by Sebastian Brant
(https://aras.org/vision-folly-american-soul)

So Lapham, too, has an eye for that side of folly that leads us blindly to destruction. From Lapham's *Age of Folly*, portraying the Fools of our Age pursuing policies for their own self-advancement or simply out of misguided patriotism, we easily progress in our Fool's Guide to Folly to the end result of this kind of folly in a scene from the film *The Fifth Element*, in which a beautiful woman from another planet embodies PEACE and LOVE (Figure 7.17).[26] Perhaps her planet is the realm of Plato's Pure Forms or Jung's archetypes. She is totally innocent of the extent to which humans will go to destroy one another in the name of some grand ideal behind which lurk far more sinister ambitions. In this scene, she gets a quick "download" lesson in the destructive folly of man.

Figure 7.17 Film Clip: *Fifth Element*
(https://aras.org/vision-folly-american-soul)

And there is a wonderfully foolish contemporary combined portrait of Kim Jong Un and Donald Trump, showing how our world leaders bamboozle us in their obsession with the pursuit of world domination for their own self-aggrandizement that will lead us inexorably into war (Figure 7.18).[27]

Figure 7.18 Trump and Kim Jong Un face swap from Google
(https://aras.org/vision-folly-american-soul)

This is, of course, a photoshopped image created in the spirit of creative folly to demonstrate the monstrousness of folly. In the modern confusion and fusion of images in our collective psyche, we witness how two apparently antagonistic world leaders have become one and the same. As mirror images of one another that blend into one another, they create a most dangerous paranoid "axis of evil" – two loose cannon madmen quite capable of triggering the most horrific folly.

Part six: conclusion

> Every other knowledge is harmful to him who does not have knowledge of goodness.
>
> Michel de Montaigne, Book I, Chapter 25[28]

It has been the goal of this Fool's Guide to Folly to offer a perspective on how to hold folly in one's heart, mind, and spirit as a guide to what is real and what is important. I believe that a sense of folly is essential for embracing life to the fullest, just as I believe that folly may well lead to the destruction of life on earth. There is the spirit of folly that makes a person vital, and there is the possession by folly that can kill civilizations. I leave you with the following questions: How can we live inside and outside of Plato's Cave? How can we live in Praise of Folly and in terror of our Age of Folly? How can we walk hand in hand with folly at our sides (or even inside us) in a way that may actually help us keep our wits, perspective, and sense of humor in a time when folly could devour everything? I end with Folly's wink from Fellini's *Juliet of the Spirits*, a tiny glimpse of an attitude that I hope each of you carries forth, both inside you and into the world from our Fool's Guide to Folly (Figure 7.19).[29]

Figure 7.19 Film Clip: *Juliet of the Spirits*, "The Wink"

(https://aras.org/vision-folly-american-soul)

Notes

1 Thomas Singer, "A Fool's Guide to Folly," in *When the Soul Remembers Itself: Ancient Greece, Modern Psyche*, ed. Thomas Singer, Jules Cashford, and Craig San Roque (London: Routledge, 2019), 11–30. By permission of the publisher.
2 Michel de Montaigne, *The Essays of Montaigne,* trans. Charles Cotton, first published 1686, Book III, Ch. XI.
3 By Permission. From Merriam-Webster.com, © 2018 by Merriam-Webster, www.merriam-webster.com/dictionary/folly.
4 C. G. Jung, *The Red Book: A Reader's Edition*, ed. Sonu Shamdasani (New York: W. W. Norton & Co., 2012), 122.
5 Nikos Kazantzakis, *Zorba the Greek* (New York: Simon and Schuster, 1952). The film of the same name was directed by Michael Cacoyannis, who also wrote the screenplay. The film was released on December 17, 1964.
6 Joseph Conrad, "The Project Gutenberg eBook of Lord Jim," eBook (accessed September 10, 2016), www.gutenberg.org/files/5658/5658-h/5658-h.htm.
7 *The Satyricon*, directed by Federico Fellini, screenplay by Federico Fellini, Bernardino Zapponi, and Brunello Rondi (Rome: Il Cinema di Fellini, released March 11, 1970).
8 Montaigne, *The Essays of Montaigne*, Book III, Ch. XIII.
9 Eric H. Warmington and Philip G. Rouse, eds., *Great Dialogues of Plato*, trans. W. H. D. Rouse (New York: Signet Classics, 1999), 316.
10 Plato, *The Republic Book VII*, ed. W. H. D. Rouse (New York: Penguin Classics, 1951), 365–401.
11 Ibid., Sections 516a–b. See also "Plato's Analogy of the Sun," which occurs near the end of *Plato's The Republic, Book VI*, ed. Benjamin Jowett (New York: The Modern Library, 1941).
12 Ibid.

13 Ibid.
14 Ibid.
15 Aristophanes, *Three Comedies* (Indianapolis, IN: Focus Publishing, 1992), lines 155–165.
16 Michel de Montaigne, quotes and images from the works of Michel de Montaigne, Project Gutenberg, www.gutenberg.org/ebooks/7551?msg=welcome_stranger.
17 All quotes from Desiderius Erasmus, *The Praise of Folly*, trans. Hoyt Hopewell Hudson, Foreword Anthony Grafton (Princeton: Princeton University Press, 2015), 16.
18 Ibid.
19 Ibid., 16–17.
20 Ibid.
21 Ibid.
22 Ibid., 19.
23 Ibid., x–xi.
24 *Amarcord*, directed by Federico Fellini, screenplay by Federico Fellini and Tonino Guerra (Rome: Warner Bros, released December 18, 1974).
25 Lewis H. Lapham, *Age of Folly: America Abandons Its Democracy* (London and New York: Verso, 2016), xii–xiii.
26 *The Fifth Element*, directed by Luc Besson, screenplay by Luc Besson and Robert Mark Kamen (Paris: Gaumont Buena Vista International, released May 9, 1997).
27 Available via Google search, "Trump and Kim Jong Un Face Swap," www. google.com/search?q=trump+and+kim+jong+un+face+swap&tbm=isch&tbo= u&source=univ&sa=X&ved=0ahUKEwjvw7qk9KPaAhVP4VQKHU-tBqQQ 7AkINA&biw=1118&bih=623#imgrc=npWG8c2UTsqaOM.
28 Michel de Montaigne, "On Schoolmasters' Learning," in *Essays*, trans. M. Screech (New York: Penguin Classics, 1991), Book I, Ch. 25, 159.
29 *Juliet of the Spirits*, directed by Federico Fellini, screenplay by Federico Fellini, Tullio Pinelli, Ennio Flaiano, and Brunello Rondi (Rome: Rizzoli Film, released November 3, 1965), https://en.wikipedia.org/wiki/Juliet_of_the_Spirits.

Index

Taylor & Francis Group
an **informa** business

Taylor & Francis eBooks

www.taylorfrancis.com

A single destination for eBooks from Taylor & Francis
with increased functionality and an improved user
experience to meet the needs of our customers.

90,000+ eBooks of award-winning academic content in
Humanities, Social Science, Science, Technology, Engineering,
and Medical written by a global network of editors and authors.

TAYLOR & FRANCIS EBOOKS OFFERS:

A streamlined
experience for
our library
customers

A single point
of discovery
for all of our
eBook content

Improved
search and
discovery of
content at both
book and
chapter level

REQUEST A FREE TRIAL
support@taylorfrancis.com

Routledge
Taylor & Francis Group

CRC Press
Taylor & Francis Group

For Product Safety Concerns and Information please contact our EU
representative GPSR@taylorandfrancis.com
Taylor & Francis Verlag GmbH, Kaufingerstraße 24, 80331 München, Germany

www.ingramcontent.com/pod-product-compliance
Lightning Source LLC
Chambersburg PA
CBHW061749270326
41928CB00011B/2435

* 9 7 8 0 3 6 7 4 3 2 6 6 9 *